D1254488

Copyright © 2010 by becker&mayer! LLC.
Text copyright © 2010 by Douglas J. Mason.

Library of Congress Cataloging-in-Publication Data available.

ISBN: 978-0-8118-6909-6

Manufactured in China.

Produced by becker&mayer! LLC, Bellevue, Washington
www.beckermayer.com

Design: Samantha Caplan
Editorial: Amelia Riedler, Matthew Taylor
Production Coordination: Diane Ross
Product Development: Jason Astrup, Peter Schumacher

10 9 8 7 6 5 4 3 2 1

Chronicle Books LLC
680 Second Street
San Francisco, CA 94107

www.chroniclebooks.com

TABLE OF CONTENTS

FOREWORD

We hope that each of you who picks up this book finds it both challenging and fun. We feel that we have captured the essence of personal cognitive growth by combining the fields of neuropsychology, business, and industry. This book represents years of work by countless patients, who have taught us the methods and strategies captured in these pages. We are in debt to the trust and confidence placed in us by those showing up on our doorstep after sustaining a life-changing injury or illness. It has been an incredible experience watching each patient's personal growth, both cognitively and spiritually. We hope that we have captured in this book the tone, the challenge, and the fun that we offer to those we are fortunate enough to work with individually.

INTRODUCTION

The most incredibly complex organ in the body has the capacity to self-repair. Your brain, science has now confirmed and continues to demonstrate, is pliable; this concept is referred to as the "plasticity" of the brain. And because the brain is pliable, you can inoculate it against future disease, injury, or dysfunction. That's right: with proper guidance, effort, and technique, you can make your brain healthier. Scientists have seen a direct correlation between level of education and delay of the onset of diseases such as Alzheimer's.

How is this possible? Because with each new memory, experience, or skill we learn, the structure of the brain actually changes. Just like running builds up your leg muscles, education and training build up your brain strength. Each piece of knowledge recorded into the brain results in the development and connection of new neurons. To give you an idea of how complex the brain is, the number of neurons in the brain is comparable to the number of stars in the Milky Way, with some estimates as high as 500 thousand million or 500 billion neurons. Groups of neurons then form neural pathways, which are interconnected to form thoughts, emotions, concepts, memories, perceptions, and our inner reality. With training, the brain will become even more complex, and the number of neural pathways will increase. Thus, the brain becomes naturally more resilient to damage because the disease or injury has a much more difficult time penetrating the millions or trillions of neural pathways.

We are literally bombarded, both by our environment and from within, with information. The average brain processes 400 trillion bits of information per second. At any given time, we are only consciously aware of about 2,000 bits. The portions of information that move into our conscious awareness are only related to our immediate environmental needs, our body, and time. Our brain works as hard to filter (or block) and sort information as it does to process conscious information. Some extremely gifted individuals, such as concert pianists or professional chess players, are not necessarily processing more than the standard 2,000 bits of information. Instead, they are processing bits more like bytes (a binary string of eight digits). So, for example, when Mozart thought about music, he thought in terms of overtures or complete compositions instead of much smaller pieces of information, such as notes or chords.

A healthy brain is able to process all these bits of information quickly and efficiently and has a great capacity for storage. And the healthier the brain, the greater its life. In other words, by increasing the density of the neural pathways, you are actually preparing your mind, intellect, and intuition to last a lifetime. Forgetfulness, and even dementia, are not a normal part of aging. Your cognitive functions should last at least until the age of 100, so 100 is the number we use for the *Brain Boot Camp* program to demonstrate your improvement. Your ultimate goal within the pages before you is to increase your brain span to 100.

Brain Boot Camp breaks down the process of increasing your brain span by working on efficiency, speed, and storage capacity within five specific categories: Executive Functions; Organization, Planning, and Logic; Memory; Language; and Visual Processing. Each of these categories works out a different part of your brain, ensuring a well-balanced approach to getting your brain in shape.

Pairing the latest scientific studies with innovative technology—your very own fun and interactive digital coach—the *Brain Boot Camp* program will guide you through an entertaining and challenging program of cognitive improvement, personal growth, and future inoculation against brain dysfunctions. Specifically tailored to your personal needs, rather than acting as a one-size-fits-all philosophy, this personalized program will get your brain fit, and working harder, faster, and more efficiently in no time.

HOW TO USE THE ELECTRONIC COACH

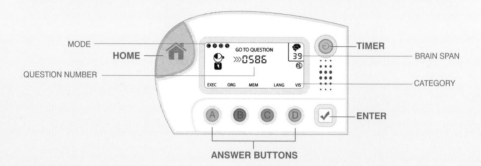

MODE

HOME

QUESTION NUMBER

GO TO QUESTION
»0586

TIMER

BRAIN SPAN

CATEGORY

39

EXEC   ORG   MEM   LANG   VIS

A   B   C   D   ✔ — ENTER

ANSWER BUTTONS

GETTING STARTED
Press the ENTER button ✔ to turn on the Coach, and begin your brain training!

DIAGNOSTIC TEST
The first time you start the Coach, you will be automatically directed to the DIAGNOSTIC TEST. This test consists of thirty randomly selected questions—six from each category—of varying difficulty to fully assess your skill level.

The Coach will automatically show a question number and its corresponding category. Possible categories are Executive Functions (EXEC); Organization, Planning, and Logic (ORG); Memory (MEM); Language (LANG); and Visual Processing (VIS). Turn to that question in the book and read it. The Coach will ask you to choose the answer. Select your answer by pressing A, B, C, or D. The display screen and accompanying sound will notify you if you are correct or incorrect.

Certain questions are timed. When you see the Timer icon ⏱, press the corresponding button on the Coach, and proceed with answering the question (see Alternative Question Types on p. 7 for more information on timed questions). Select your answer by pressing A, B, C, or D.

After you take the DIAGNOSTIC TEST, the Coach will show your overall BRAIN SPAN score and your scores within each category. Use the A and D buttons to cycle through each category score. Scores range from a low of 0 to a high of 100. Your scores can be checked at any time by choosing the BRAIN SPAN mode. The results of the test will give the Coach the information needed to create a personalized training regimen just for you!

HOW IT WORKS
The Coach tracks your progress by remembering your answers for the last ten questions in each category, weighing the difficulty of the question and how accurately (and sometimes how quickly) you answered each question. If you answer questions correctly, the Coach will challenge you by asking consecutively harder questions. Generally, if your category score is 0–44, you will be asked easy questions; 45–78, medium difficulty questions; and 79–100, hard questions. You must advance to the most difficult questions in the book and be able to answer them correctly before you can obtain the highest BRAIN SPAN. Try reaching a perfect score of 100!

HOME
From the HOME screen you can choose the TRAINING MODE (COACH, PRACTICE, DIAGNOSTIC, or BRAIN SPAN). You can return to the main menu at any time by pressing the HOME button 🏠.

TRAINING MODES
CHOOSING THE TRAINING MODE
- Use the A and D buttons to cycle through the modes until the one you wish to select appears on the screen.
- Press ENTER ✔ to select the mode.

COACH: In this mode, the Coach will select specific questions for you based on your current BRAIN SPAN. The goal

is to strengthen the areas in which you are weaker and increase your overall BRAIN SPAN score. While in COACH mode, your BRAIN SPAN continually updates with each question you answer and is shown in the upper right corner of the display screen.

Once you are in COACH mode:
- Use the A and D buttons to cycle between OVERALL and ISOLATED.
- In OVERALL mode, the Coach will select questions across all categories, with difficult questions from areas in which you are strong and easier questions from areas in which you need more training.
- In ISOLATED mode, you can ask the Coach to train you using questions from one specific category. Use the A and D buttons to cycle between categories.
- Press ENTER ☑ to make your selection.

PRACTICE: In this mode, you will have the ability to select questions and practice in any category you want at your own pace. Your BRAIN SPAN is *not* affected while you are in PRACTICE mode.

Once you are in PRACTICE mode:
- Use the A and D buttons to cycle between RANDOM and USER SELECT.
- RANDOM mode will give you randomly selected questions from throughout the book.
- In USER SELECT mode, you can select specific questions. Press ENTER ☑ to accept the question number displayed, or enter the number of the question you wish to answer by pressing A for each 1,000 digit, B for each 100, C for each 10, and D for single digits.
- Press ENTER ☑ to make your selection.

DIAGNOSTIC TEST: After the initial test, select this mode only if you want to reset your BRAIN SPAN and start fresh. After selecting this mode, you will be asked to confirm if you want to proceed. Once the test is complete, your new BRAIN SPAN score will replace your previous score.

BRAIN SPAN: In this mode, you will be able to see your overall BRAIN SPAN score and your progress in each category. Use the A and D buttons to cycle through your scores for each category.

ALTERNATIVE QUESTION TYPES

TIMED: Some questions give a set amount of time to review an image, figure, etc., and some are meant for you to answer as quickly as you can.

For set-timed questions, the book will tell you how much time you have to review a figure, image, or another item. Begin by pressing the Timer ☾ on the Coach, then review the item. Answer the question by pressing A, B, C, or D as fast as you can before the Timer ☾ rings.

For stopwatch questions, the book will tell you to press the Timer ☾ on the Coach and answer as quickly as you can. You will have up to three minutes to choose an answer, but the quickness of your response is as important as which answer you choose. Select your answer by pressing A, B, C,

or D. If you do not choose an answer after three minutes, the Coach will automatically register the answer as incorrect and proceed to the next question.

AURAL: Some questions will require you to listen for different tones. For these questions, the Coach will ask you to press Enter ☑ to hear a SOUND KEY. The SOUND KEY will play four tones, and as each tone is played, a number on the display screen will be shown. You must associate each tone with the correct number. Then the Coach will ask you to press Enter ☑ to hear the QUESTION SEQUENCE. Use this sequence to answer the question.

VISUAL: Some questions will require you to recognize visual patterns and sequences. For these questions, the Coach will display a sequence of letters and/or numbers. The Coach will then ask you to press Enter ☑ to see the QUESTION SEQUENCE. Use this sequence to answer the question.

ADDITIONAL FEATURES
- The display will go to sleep after three minutes idle, but can be awakened by pressing any button. The Coach will resume where you left off, remembering the last question asked, the mode selected, and your current BRAIN SPAN score.
- To manually turn off the Coach, hold down Enter ☑ for three seconds.
- When you are answering questions, the category for the displayed question will be indicated at the bottom of the display screen.
- When you are choosing modes and answering questions, the letters "C," "P," "D," and "S," corresponding to the different modes, will be indicated in the upper left corner of the display screen.
- The Coach will encourage you and give feedback with scrolling messages as you answer questions. Press any button at any time to skip a scrolling message.
- The audio can be turned off and on at any time by holding down the Timer ☾ Button. The display screen will show a speaker icon ◀ when the audio is on or a speaker-off icon 🔇 when the audio is off. When the audio is turned off, the Coach will *not* ask Aural questions.

BATTERIES
The Coach uses three AG13 button cell batteries. If the Coach does not turn on, you may need to replace the batteries. To do so, you must first remove the screw from the side of the Coach. Once the screw is removed, slide the battery cover off, replace the old batteries with the new ones, and slide the cover back onto the Coach. Insert the screw, and tighten.

EXECUTIVE FUNCTIONS

ATTENTION & COGNITIVE PROCESSING SPEED

E xecutive Functions are seated in the frontal lobes of the brain. Essentially, the frontal lobes serve as the brain's horsepower and integrate all other brain functions, allowing us to focus, make decisions, manage, and direct.

Attention is the most critical Executive Function for all other cognitive processes—you can think of it as the foundation of cognitive functioning. Attention occurs when you are consciously focused on a task—not only are you present physically, but your mind is also attuned to each phase of the task at hand.

Frequently, like when you are driving to a familiar place, you are not actively attending to the task. In this state, your attention becomes "passive" because your mind is able to proceed without the level of focus that a new task requires. You may instead be thinking about chores at home, a meeting at work, or a problem you are experiencing. When your attention drifts away from the task at hand, you may startle when the current task recaptures your attention, say when the car in front you slams on the brakes. At that point, you return to "active" attention.

In addition to the passive and active designations, Attention can be broken down into five types: Normal, Concentration, Selective, Alternating, and Divided. Normal attention is consciously focusing on a single task. Concentration is the act of sustaining attention and is usually required when performing a task just beyond your capability. Reading, for example, is an act of concentration or sustained attention. Selective attention is the ability to focus on one activity while blocking out some other form of stimulation. Perhaps your spouse likes to watch TV at night while you like to read. Your ability to "ignore" the television while concentrating on your book would be an example of selective attention. Alternating attention represents the ability to switch your attention between two tasks. Using the same example, maybe you listen to the fragments of the television program that pique your interest while you continue to read your book. Finally, Divided attention is accomplished when you perform multiple tasks simultaneously. An example would be folding laundry while listening to your child read from a book.

In addition to Attention, Cognitive Processing Speed is another important Executive Function. Cognitive Processing Speed is the speed and efficiency with which you accomplish a challenge. It is essentially how fast you think. Within your brain, electrical signals travel through neural networks. The faster these signals travel, the more information the brain can process in any given amount of time. Thus, Cognitive Processing Speed measures how responsive your brain is. The speed of your brain can have a profound impact on your decision-making and intellectual abilities.

Within this chapter, the Coach will push your cognitive abilities to the limit, to stretch your capacity in terms of enhancing the speed at which you are able to move large amounts of data accurately. You will also refine your ability to successfully attend to both mundane and complicated tasks.

FIGURE 1

0001. How many items in Fig. 1 can fix mistakes?

    A. Three   **C.** None
    B. Two   **D.** One

0002. How many items in Fig. 1 are holding or can hold paper?

    A. Nine   **C.** Seven
    B. Five   **D.** Six

0003. How many items in Fig. 1 are edible?

    A. One   **C.** Two
    B. Three   **D.** Five

0004. How many items in Fig. 1 have numbers on them?

    A. One   **C.** Two

    B. Four   **D.** Three

0005. How many items in Fig. 1 start with the letter "C"?

    A. Four   **C.** Five

    B. Six   **D.** Three

FIGURE 2

0006. Which element shown in Fig. 2 above is *not* shown in Fig. 3 below?

    A. جْٔ   **C.** جْٔ

    B. جْ   **D.** جْ

0007. Which element is shown in Fig. 2 twice?

    A. ە   **C.** عِ

    B. جْ   **D.** جْ

0008. Which element is shown in Fig. 3 below but *not* in Fig. 2 above?

    A. ت   **C.** د

    B. ح   **D.** !

0009. Which of the following elements appears twice in Fig. 3 below?

    A. ؤْ   **C.** عِ

    B. وْ   **D.** جْ

FIGURE 3

FIGURE 4

6	9	8	4	5	2	3	5	7	9	0	2	1	7	5
2	6	5	3	2	4	7	9	4	7	3	4	8	4	1
6	5	3	2	5	9	0	1	7	6	4	2	5	0	6
8	3	5	2	6	7	1	9	3	5	8	0	2	4	9
3	5	8	1	7	4	2	3	5	1	9	4	7	0	3
7	1	4	7	9	0	3	6	8	2	9	6	8	3	2
6	9	3	8	6	5	2	0	3	9	4	2	0	4	1
7	8	4	2	7	0	4	8	5	8	3	1	7	6	4
2	0	9	3	6	5	2	7	6	0	4	7	2	5	0
5	6	0	2	5	9	3	5	8	3	1	0	8	6	2
7	0	9	3	2	7	4	1	9	2	0	6	3	9	1
6	5	3	0	5	8	3	1	2	6	4	2	8	7	2
3	8	4	7	1	3	9	2	7	1	0	4	3	4	1
0	2	5	8	0	6	3	9	5	2	5	0	8	3	5
2	6	8	9	6	1	4	7	2	0	4	7	1	8	3

USE YOUR ATTENTION WISELY

The more complex the type of attention, the more energy is required. Attention functions fall under the conservation principle: there is only a limited amount of energy that we can expend before we become fatigued. So spend your attention energy wisely. If you don't need to multi-task and can control distractions or interruptions, then do so. You'll find that you are less stressed and more proficient as a result.

0010. How many 6's are in Fig. 4?

    A. Twenty   **C.** Twenty-one
    B. Nineteen   **D.** Twenty-three

0011. How many 9's are in Fig. 4?

    A. Seventeen   **C.** Nineteen
    B. Fifteen   **D.** Sixteen

0012. How many 8's are in Fig. 4?

    A. Twenty   **C.** Eighteen
    B. Twenty-one   **D.** Nineteen

0013. How many 3's are in Fig. 4?

    A. Twenty-nine   **C.** Twenty-seven
    B. Twenty-five   **D.** Twenty-six

0014. Which number appears most frequently in Fig. 4?

    A. 3   **C.** 5
    B. 2   **D.** 4

0015. Which number appears least often in Fig. 4?

    A. 6   **C.** 1
    B. 9   **D.** 4

0016. How many times does 6 immediately precede 9 horizontally in Fig. 4?

    A. Three   **C.** Two
    B. One   **D.** Zero

0017. How many times does 6 immediately precede 9 vertically in Fig. 4?

    A. Two   **C.** One
    B. Zero   **D.** Three

0018. How many times does 0 immediately follow 8 horizontally in Fig. 4?

    A. Three   **C.** One
    B. Zero   **D.** Two

0019. How many times does 2 immediately precede 5 vertically in Fig. 4?

    A. Two   **C.** Zero
    B. Three   **D.** One

0020. Use the Coach to hear and see the sound key and question sequence, then answer the question. [STOP] Which of the following matches the sound sequence?

    A. 2231   **C.** 2213
    B. 2132   **D.** 2123

FIGURE 5

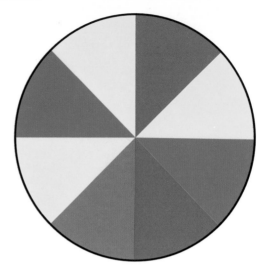

0021. If you were to spin the wheel in Fig. 5, what would be your chances of landing on red?

   A. 1:8   **C.** 1:4
   B. 1:2   **D.** 2:2

0022. If you were to spin the wheel in Fig. 5, on which color would you be most likely to land?

   A. Blue   **C.** Yellow
   B. Red   **D.** Green

0023. What percentage of the wheel in Fig. 5 is not blue?

   A. 25 percent **C.** 75 percent
   B. 50 percent **D.** 80 percent

0024. It's 2010 and you are forty-one years old. You got your driving permit when you were sixteen. What year did you begin driving?

   A. 1969   **C.** 1975
   B. 1985   **D.** 1995

0025. Which of the following Roman numerals is equivalent to 2,049?

A. MMXLIX   **C.** MMXLVIIII

B. MMXCIX   **D.** MMXXXXVIIII

0026. Which triangle is different from the other triangles?

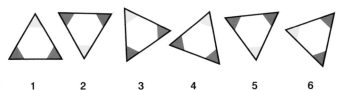

1   2   3   4   5   6

A. Triangle 2   **C.** Triangle 6

B. Triangle 4   **D.** Triangle 3

0027. Use the Coach to hear and see the sound key and question sequence, then answer the question. [STOP] Which of the following matches the sound sequence?

A. 2424   **C.** 1212

B. 2323   **D.** 1313

0028. Use the Coach to hear and see the sound key and question sequence, then answer the question. [STOP] Which of the following matches the sound sequence?

A. 2123   **C.** 2134

B. 2143   **D.** 2413

0029. Use the Coach to hear and see the sound key and question sequence, then answer the question. [STOP] Which of the following matches the sound sequence, but in reverse?

A. 1432   **C.** 3214

B. 1423   **D.** 4132

0030. Press the ↻ on the Coach, then solve the equation as quickly as you can. The value of each letter corresponds to its placement in the alphabet, i.e. A=1, Z=26, etc.

$$(N-L) \times O =$$

A. 28   **C.** 25

B. 30   **D.** 32

EXECUTIVE

0021–0030

15

FIGURE 6

	1	2	3	4	5	6	7
1	hld	zch	dbq	hex	Hd	dhu	khz
2	dlg	gdz	gqb	egd	Hdg	quw	kzg
3	etl	etc	bte	dtx	The	tuw	ktz
4	vni	zvcc	vbq	xvi	Dhv	uvi	ziv
5	nml	clm	qbl	mix	Hdl	wmlu	kml
6	ylb	yze	qby	bye	Dhy	wuy	zyk
7	lpn	cpb	qpb	xpc	Dph	upc	kpc

0031. Which cell in Fig. 6 includes three letters that are also commonly used as an abbreviation? Answers are in Row, Column order.

    A. 3, 2   **C.** 2, 3
    B. 6, 4   **D.** 5, 4

0032. Which cell in Fig. 6 contains a common shape of a nut or bolt? Answers are in Row, Column order.

    A. 3, 5   **C.** 1, 4
    B. 4, 4   **D.** 7, 6

0033. Which cell in Fig. 6 contains an article (a part of speech)? Answers are in Row, Column order.

    A. 6, 4   **C.** 1, 4
    B. 3, 5   **D.** 5, 3

0034. Which cell in Fig. 6 contains the number 16? Answers are in Row, Column order.

    A. 4, 6   **C.** 4, 4
    B. 2, 1   **D.** 3, 1

0035. Which cell in Fig. 6 contains a three-letter word that is also a closing or valediction? Answers are in Row, Column order.

    A. 7, 6   **C.** 4, 6
    B. 6, 4   **D.** 7, 5

0036. Which cell in Fig. 6 is an abbreviation for a type of nurse? Answers are in Row, Column order.

    A. 1, 7   **C.** 6, 7
    B. 2, 3   **D.** 7, 1

0037. Which cell in Fig. 6 contains another name for a bar code? Answers are in Row, Column order.

    A. 3, 2   **C.** 6, 3
    B. 7, 6   **D.** 6, 7

0038. Which cell in Fig. 6 has four letters in it? Answers are in Row, Column order.

    A. 6, 5   **C.** 2, 7
    B. 5, 6   **D.** 3, 7

0039. Which cell in Fig. 6 has two letters in it? Answers are in Row, Column order.

    A. 5, 1   **C.** 1, 4
    B. 1, 5   **D.** 7, 4

0040. Which cell in Fig. 6 contains another name for a curse or evil spell? Answers are in Row, Column order.

    A. 3, 4   **C.** 5, 4
    B. 1, 5   **D.** 1, 4

0041. Use the Coach to hear and see the sound key and question sequence, then answer the question. [STOP] What was the third sound in the sequence?

    A. 2   **C.** 1
    B. 4   **D.** 3

COCOA MAY REDUCE DEMENTIA

Recent studies indicate that flavonols found in cocoa increase blood flow to the brain. While there is no direct evidence that this correlates to a reduction in dementia or ischemic activity, it is known that those with dementia have less than average brain blood flow. Thus, it is speculated that cocoa may play a positive role in reducing the brain's susceptibility to dementia.

0042. Use the Coach to hear and see the sound key and question sequence, then answer the question. [stop] Which sound was repeated most frequently in the sequence?

A. 1   **C.** 3
B. 2   **D.** 4

0043. Use the Coach to hear and see the sound key and question sequence, then answer the question. [stop] Which sound was *not* included in the sequence?

A. 3   **C.** 2
B. 1   **D.** 4

0044. Use the Coach to hear and see the sound key and question sequence, then answer the question. [stop] Which sound in the sequence was *not* included in the sound key and is heard when the timer ends when using this book?

A. 1   **C.** 3
B. 2   **D.** 5

0045. Use the Coach to hear and see the sound key and question sequence, then answer the question. [stop] How many times was sound "A" used in the sequence?

A. Four   **C.** Three
B. Two   **D.** Five

0046. Use the Coach to hear and see the sound key and question sequence, then answer the question. [stop] Which sound would correctly complete the pattern?

A. 3   **C.** 4
B. 2   **D.** 1

0047. Use the Coach to hear and see the sound key and question sequence, then answer the question. [stop] Which sound would be the first sound in the pattern?

A. 2   **C.** 4
B. 3   **D.** 1

0048. Use the Coach to hear and see the sound key and question sequence, then answer the question. [STOP] Which sound was played first in the sequence?

A. 3   **C.** 4
B. 2   **D.** 1

0049. Use the Coach to hear and see the sound key and question sequence, then answer the question. [STOP] Which sound was *not* played after sound 4?

A. 2   **C.** 1
B. 3   **D.** 4

0050. Use the Coach to hear and see the sound key and question sequence, then answer the question. [STOP] Which of the following matches the sound sequence?

A. 13241   **C.** 133214
B. 133241   **D.** 133243

0051. Use the Coach to hear and see the sound key and question sequence, then answer the question. [STOP] What are the correct keys for this pattern?

A. 112212   **C.** 112121
B. 121121   **D.** 122122

0052. Use the Coach to hear and see the sound key and question sequence, then answer the question. [STOP] Which of the following matches the sound sequence, but in reverse?

A. 412324   **C.** 412342
B. 413224   **D.** 413242

0053. Press the ↻ on the Coach, then solve the equation as quickly as you can. The value of each letter corresponds to its placement in the alphabet, i.e. A=1, Z=26, etc.

$(F+X)/E =$

A. 6   **C.** 10
B. 5   **D.** 4

EXECUTIVE

0042 – 0053

JAVA JUICE?

Caffeine is classified as a drug because it serves to stimulate the central nervous system. Many of us are dependent on our morning coffee and afternoon cola to keep us awake and alert. While it is true that caffeine contains properties that stimulate our central nervous system, it is also generally considered a short-term fix. Your body quickly adapts to the use, and the threshold for "effect" increases rapidly. Caffeine does improve alertness and will provide a burst of energy. But excess consumption may result in irritability and anxiety, at which point the consumption of caffeine becomes counterproductive in our search for mental efficiency. It is also addictive. Your body will become dependent on the usage and will suffer withdrawal symptoms such as fatigue. Caffeine may be beneficial in improving our concentration short-term but should be used in moderation long-term.

FIGURE 7

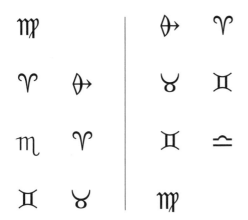

0054. Which symbol shown on the left side of Fig. 7 is *not* shown on the right side?

    A. ♏   **C.** ♍
    B. ⚕   **D.** ♌

0055. Which symbol is shown twice on the left side of Fig. 7?

    A. ♑   **C.** ♈
    B. ♏   **D.** ♉

0056. Which symbol shown on the right side of Fig. 7 is *not* shown on the left side?

    A. ♊   **C.** ♈
    B. ♉   **D.** ♎

0057. Which symbol is shown twice on the right side of Fig. 7?

    A. ♊   **C.** ⚕
    B. ♌   **D.** ♍

0058. Use the Coach to see the question sequence, then answer the question. [STOP] What was the fourth digit?

    A. 5   **C.** 1
    B. 7   **D.** 2

FIGURE 8

	1	2	3	4	5	6	7
1	khul	hutl	ulfh	sdhu	Pnht	hslh	nohu
2	nmak	hkna	hkan	dnka	Pnka	fsnk	goka
3	ehmr	herb	ureb	dger	Pner	fsrb	erog
4	rihn	hntr	rihn	grih	Rinvp	fsri	kiog
5	lhms	nlst	lshu	lsdg	Lsnv	hfls	nosh
6	emhi	hen	uhie	endg	Neiv	iefs	gien
7	emhy	hndy	dhfy	ghds	Nvdy	sfyh	gdyn

0059. Which individual cell in Fig. 8 contains two of the same letters? Answers are in Row, Column order.

A. 5, 4   **C.** 6, 1

B. 1, 3   **D.** 1, 6

0060. Which cell in Fig. 8 only contains three letters? Answers are in Row, Column order.

A. 3, 6   **C.** 2, 3

B. 7, 6   **D.** 6, 2

0061. Which two cells in Fig. 8 are the same? Answers are in Row, Column order.

A. 4, 1; 4, 3   **C.** 5, 2; 3, 4

B. 3, 4; 3, 1   **D.** 6, 3; 7, 1

0062. In which cell in Fig. 8 can you unscramble the letters to spell the word "vein"? Answers are in Row, Column order.

A. 1, 2   **C.** 5, 1

B. 7, 1   **D.** 6, 5

0063. Which cell in Fig. 8 contains the word "herb"? Answers are in Row, Column order.

    A. 4, 2   **C.** 2, 3
    B. 4, 6   **D.** 3, 2

0064. Which cell in Fig. 8 spells another name for a female chicken? Answers are in Row, Column order.

    A. 6, 2   **C.** 5, 3
    B. 2, 6   **D.** 4, 6

0065. In which cell in Fig. 8 can you unscramble the letters and spell the word "lush"? Answers are in Row, Column order.

    A. 3, 5   **C.** 2, 6
    B. 5, 3   **D.** 6, 2

0066. In which cell in Fig. 8 can you change one letter and spell the word "frog"? Answers are in Row, Column order.

    A. 3, 6   **C.** 7, 4
    B. 7, 3   **D.** 3, 7

0067. Which cell in Fig. 8 contains the letters "k," "n," "d," and "a" (in any order)? Answers are in Row, Column order.

    A. 3, 6   **C.** 4, 2
    B. 3, 4   **D.** 2, 4

0068. Which cell in Fig. 8 contains five letters? Answers are in Row, Column order.

    A. 1, 3   **C.** 6, 7
    B. 5, 4   **D.** 4, 5

0069. What is the sum total of the numbers in this list?

87341208956179286780927410 83748542

    A. 156   **C.** 178
    B. 165   **D.** 162

FIGURE 9

	1	2	3	4	5	6	7
1	8yf!	#3mf	G5!f	*e5f	U7f!	D9*u7	4#!5
2	3gy*	23g)	^5g3	E3)g	&3g)	*93g	3g#m
3	8$*y	M8$i	8i5g	5*$8	g8$7	8d9*	l8#m
4	4*r@y	24r@	^@r4	@re*	@r7&	94r@	4rm#
5	N18y	N12m	Ng5^	*%n1	N7&%	9n1	#n%1
6	4fy8	#4fm	4>^5	>f45	7&4f	4>*f	>4f#
7	1*38	2w+m	^gw+	+*w7	7w7&	7w9*	Mw7+

0070. How many cells in Fig. 9 contain two letters in them?

    A. Twenty-two   **C.** Twenty-one
    B. Twenty-three   **D.** Twenty

0071. Which cells in Fig. 9 contain five characters? Answers are in Row, Column order.

    A. 5, 6; 4, 1   **C.** 6, 1; 1, 4
    B. 1, 3; 1, 6   **D.** 1, 6; 4, 1

0072. Which cell in Fig. 9 contains three numbers? Answers are in Row, Column order.

    A. 6, 1   **C.** 2, 2
    B. 7, 1   **D.** 3, 2

0073. Which cell in Fig. 9 contains the same number twice? Answers are in Row, Column order.

    A. 7, 5   **C.** 7, 2
    B. 5, 7   **D.** 6, 2

0074. Which cells in Fig. 9 do *not* contain any letters? Answers are in Row, Column order.

    A. 3, 6; 7, 1   **C.** 4, 5; 6, 3
    B. 2, 5; 1, 7   **D.** 6, 3; 7, 1

0075. Which cell in Fig. 9 contains the "&" symbol and the number 3? Answers are in Row, Column order.

    A. 2, 3   **C.** 2, 4
    B. 2, 5   **D.** 2, 6

0076. How many cells in Fig. 9 contain the "＾" symbol?

    A. Three   **C.** Four
    B. Five   **D.** Six

0077. Which cell in Fig. 9 contains the combination "g8$7"? Answers are in Row, Column order.

    A. 3, 5   **C.** 4, 6
    B. 5, 3   **D.** 7, 1

0078. How many cells in Fig. 9 contain two different symbols?

    A. Nineteen   **C.** Sixteen
    B. Seventeen   **D.** Fifteen

0079. Which cell in Fig. 9 contains only three characters? Answers are in Row, Column order.

    A. 5, 4   **C.** 5, 6
    B. 5, 3   **D.** 6, 5

0080. Press the ↻ on the Coach, then solve the equation as quickly as you can. The value of each letter corresponds to its placement in the alphabet, i.e. A=1, Z=26, etc.

$Y+D-I =$

    A. S   **C.** T
    B. R   **D.** Q

HELPFUL HINTS

1. Read the instructions. If you think you don't need instructions, read them twice!

2. Keep a notepad handy to record your responses, especially when asked to count characters. You may need that information to answer another question.

3. Have a calculator handy.

4. If you start feeling frustrated or you're fatigued, take a break. Even a few minutes away can give you a fresh perspective.

FIGURE 10

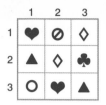

FIGURE 11

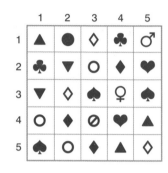

LEGEND

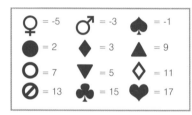

0081. Using the Legend for values, which row in Fig. 10 has the greatest numerical value?

    A. Row 3
    B. Rows 1 and 2 are equal
    C. Row 2
    D. Row 1

0082. Using the Legend for values, what is the value of Row 3 in Fig. 10?

    A. 35   **C.** 41
    B. 33   **D.** 39

0083. Using the Legend for values, what is the value of Column 2 in Fig. 10?

    A. 35   **C.** 33
    B. 41   **D.** 31

0084. Using the Legend for values, which row(s) and column(s) in Fig. 10 have the same value?

    A. Row 1, Column 2
    B. Row 2, Column 3; Row 1, Column 2
    C. Row 1, Column 2; Row 2, Column 3; Row 3, Column 1
    D. Row 3, Column 1; Row 1, Column 2

0085. Using the Legend for values, which column has the greatest numerical value in Fig. 10?

    A. Columns 1 and 3 are equal
    B. Column 3
    C. Column 1
    D. Column 2

0086. Which symbols occur once in Fig. 11?

    A. ●, ♂, ⊘, ♀   **C.** ●, ♂, ♀
    B. ▼, ●, ⊘, ♀   **D.** ⊘, ♂, ♠, ●

0087. Using the Legend for values, which row or column has the greatest numerical value in Fig. 11?

    A. Row 4   **C.** Row 2
    B. Column 3   **D.** Column 1

0088. Using the Legend for values, which row or column has the least numerical value in Fig. 11?

    A. Row 1   **C.** Row 4
    B. Row 3   **D.** Column 2

0089. Using the Legend for values, what is the value for Column 3 in Fig. 11?

    A. 34   **C.** 26
    B. 33   **D.** 28

0090. Using the Legend for values, which symbol in Fig. 11 has the greatest numerical value?

    A. ♣   **C.** ●
    B. ♥   **D.** ♠

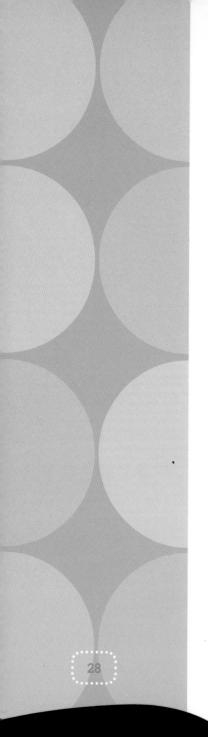

FIGURE 12

	1	2	3	4
1	♂	▼	♥	●
2	▲	O	♣	◇
3	◆	♀	♠	⊘
4	●	◆	O	♠

LEGEND

♀ = -5	♂ = -3	♠ = -1
● = 2	◆ = 3	▲ = 9
O = 7	▼ = 5	◇ = 11
⊘ = 13	♣ = 15	♥ = 17

0091. Using the Legend for values, determine the total value of each row in Fig. 12 by multiplying the first column's first cell by the second column's first cell, adding that value to Column 3's first cell, and finally subtracting that value from Column 4's first cell. Repeat for each row. Which row has the greatest numerical value?

A. Row 1   **C.** Row 2
B. Row 3   **D.** Row 4

0092. Using the Legend for values, determine the total value of each row in Fig. 12 by multiplying the first column's first cell by the second column's first cell, adding that value to Column 3's first cell, and finally subtracting that value from Column 4's first cell. Repeat for each row. Which row has the lowest numerical value?

A. Row 4   **C.** Row 3
B. Row 2   **D.** Row 1

0093. Add the value of all of the symbols in Fig. 12. What is the numerical value of the grid?

A. 94   **C.** 88
B. 84   **D.** 90

0094. Using the Legend for values, determine the total value of each row in Fig. 12 by multiplying the first column's first cell by the second column's first cell, adding that value to Column 3's first cell, and finally subtracting that value from Column 4's first cell. Repeat for each row. If you could rearrange the symbols in Row 3, which arrangement would give you the greatest value?

A. ♀,♠,♦,⊘   C. ⊘,♠,♀,♦
B. ♦,♠,⊘,♀   D. ♦,⊘,♠,♀

0095. Using the Legend for values, determine the total value of each row in Fig. 12 by multiplying the first column's first cell by the second column's first cell, adding that value to Column 3's first cell, and finally subtracting that value from Column 4's first cell. Repeat for each row. If the ● symbol changed to a ▲ symbol, and the ♦ symbol changed to a ◊ symbol, which row would have the greatest value?

A. Row 1   C. Row 4
B. Row 2   D. Row 3

0096. Use the Coach to see the question sequence, then answer the question. [STOP] What did all of the digits have in common?

A. Each number is only two numbers apart from the previous number
B. They are in numerical order
C. They are in reverse numerical order
D. They are all odd numbers

0097. Use the Coach to see the question sequence, then answer the question. [STOP] What do all of the digits have in common?

A. They are all even numbers and multiples of two
B. They are all odd numbers
C. They are in numerical order
D. They are in reverse numerical order

0098. Use the Coach to see the question sequence, then answer the question. [STOP] What is the numerical order of the digits?

A. 12689   C. 25689
B. 12789   D. 13789

EXECUTIVE

0091–
0098

29

HELLO, I'M ...

Are you, like many others, "terrible" at remembering names? Truth be told, do you really and truly actively pay attention to a person's name when you are introduced for the first time? Or are you more aware of the impression you are about to make or the conversation at hand or who else is around? Chances are, your attention is divided among so many other things that you are not concentrating on the person's name and thus have no chance to encode it in your memory. So, the next time you are introduced to someone, truly pay attention—repeat the name in your mind, associate the name, with someone you already know by that name, or rhyme it with another word—be creative. You will be amazed at how many names you'll start to remember.

0099. Use the Coach to see the question sequence, then answer the question. [STOP] What is the order of the numbers from greatest to least?

A. 76532   C. 87532
B. 87321   D. 87231

0100. Use the Coach to see the question sequence, then answer the question. [STOP] In which order did the numbers appear?

A. 9176240   C. 9176204
B. 9172640   D. 9172604

0101. Use the Coach to see the question sequence, then answer the question. [STOP] What is the reverse order of how the digits appeared?

A. 9182574   C. 9185274
B. 9185247   D. 9182547

0102. Use the Coach to see the question sequence, then answer the question. [STOP] What is the sum of the digits?

A. 23   C. 25
B. 24   D. 26

0103. Use the Coach to see the question sequence, then answer the question. [STOP] What was the middle, or third, digit?

A. 5   C. 7
B. 9   D. 2

0104. Use the Coach to see the question sequence, then answer the question. [STOP] What is the numerical order of the digits?

A. 1234568   C. 123689
B. 1234689   D. 123469

0105. You have 7 ½ gallons of milk, 3 ¼ gallons of juice, and 6 ¾ gallons of iced tea. How many ounces of fluid do you have?

A. 560   C. 1,120
B. 2,240   D. 1,088

EXECUTIVE

0099–
0105

31

FIGURE 13

0106. Which object appears in Fig. 13 a multiple of three times?

    A. Bus   **C.** Raft

    B. Hot-air balloon   **D.** Fire truck

0107. Which of the items in Fig. 13 appears most frequently?

    A. Raft   **C.** Canoe

    B. Bus   **D.** Police car

0108. If you categorize the items in Fig. 13 by Land, Sea, Air, or Foot, which category has the most items?

    A. Land   **C.** Air

    B. Foot   **D.** Sea

FIGURE 14

DJLWX

0109. Which of the following is *not* pictured in Fig. 13?

    A. Blimp   **C.** Ambulance
    B. Jeep   **D.** Skateboard

0110. Which of the following items all have an even number of appearances in Fig. 13?

    A. Fire truck, Hot-air balloon, Jet, Canoe
    B. Jet, Police car, Gondola
    C. Hot-air balloon, Jet, Wagon
    D. Hot-air balloon, Police car, Canoe, Jet

0111. Use the Coach to see the question sequence, then answer the question. [STOP] What was the third digit, reading from left to right?

    A. 8   **C.** 7
    B. 2   **D.** 4

0112. Use the Coach to see the question sequence, then answer the question. [STOP] What was the fifth digit, reading from left to right?

    A. 3   **C.** 5
    B. 8   **D.** 6

0113. What do the following items have in common?

Eggs, Flowers, Pencils, Apostles

    A. Things that can be found on a table
    B. Products of other things
    C. Living things
    D. Things that come by the dozen

0114. Use the Coach to see the question sequence, then answer the question. [STOP] What is the reverse numerical order of the digits?

    A. 24019   **C.** 42091
    B. 24091   **D.** 24901

EXECUTIVE

0106–
0114

33

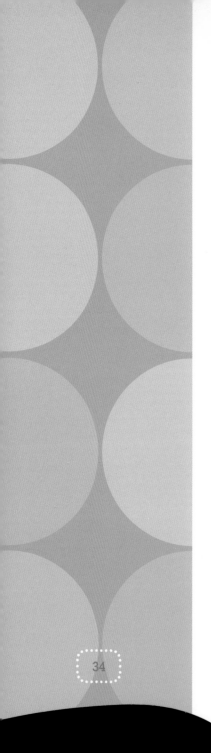

FIGURE 15

John and his friends are measuring their heights. Sally is shorter than John. Ben is taller than Sally, but shorter than John. Elizabeth is shorter than Sally.

0115. Use the Coach to see the question sequence, then answer the question. [STOP] In which order did the numbers appear?

    A. 4392518   **C.** 4395218
    B. 4395281   **D.** 4392581

0116. Use the Coach to see the question sequence, then answer the question. [STOP] In which order did the numbers appear?

    A. 06483   **C.** 06438
    B. 06843   **D.** 06834

0117. Use the Coach to see the question sequence, then answer the question. [STOP] In which order did the numbers appear?

    A. 25983   **C.** 25389
    B. 25893   **D.** 25938

0118. Use the Coach to see the question sequence, then answer the question. [STOP] What was the middle digit?

    A. 6   **C.** 3
    B. 2   **D.** 1

0119. Use the Coach to see the question sequence, then answer the question. [STOP] Which number in the sequence had the lowest value?

    A. 2   **C.** 3
    B. 0   **D.** 1

0120. Read Fig. 15. Who is the tallest person in the group?

    A. Sally   **C.** John
    B. Ben   **D.** Elizabeth

0121. Read Fig. 15. Who is the shortest person in the group?

    A. Sally   **C.** Elizabeth
    B. Ben   **D.** John

0122. Glance at the letters in Fig. 14 on p. 33 very briefly. Which of the letters from the figure are excluded from the grid below?

    W L D X A
    A W C X L
    D A W L X
    L W D A X

    A. W   **C.** J
    B. D   **D.** X

0123. Glance at the letters in Fig. 14 on p. 33 very briefly. Which of the following letters was *not* included?

    A. X   **C.** A
    B. W   **D.** L

0124. Glance at the letters in Fig. 14 on p. 33 very briefly. How many total letters were shown?

    A. Five   **C.** Four
    B. Six   **D.** Seven

0125. Use the Coach to see the question sequence, then answer the question. [STOP] What were the digits in the order they appeared?

    A. 25983   **C.** 25389
    B. 25893   **D.** 25938

0126. Press the ↻ on the Coach, then answer the question as quickly as you can. The value of each letter corresponds to its placement in the alphabet, i.e. A=1, Z=26, etc.

A+D+G =

    A. J   **C.** L
    B. 9   **D.** 11

BIOFEEDBACK

Biofeedback is a tool used to improve awareness of your body's physiological response to stress, which you can use to modify or retrain that response. Biofeedback can be simple—like measuring the changes in your heart rate during a variety of tasks, or complex, such as taking EKG-like measurements of brain waves. Simple or complex, the goal is to retrain your brain's response to stress. Cognitively, you want to instruct your brain to relax during increased stress, so that you can focus and concentrate on the task at hand.

0127. In the diagram below, one flower is different from all of the others. How is it different?

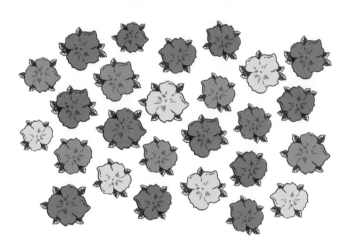

A. The leaves are different sizes
B. The center is a different size
C. It has six leaves
D. All the flowers are the same

0128. What do the following items have in common?

Iron, Titanium, Nickel, Zinc

A. Rare metals
B. Located in the fourth period of the Periodic Table of Elements
C. Nontoxic items
D. Vitamins

0129. Your password must have eight characters. There must be at least two digits, however, they cannot be at the beginning or the end. No more than two letters can be consecutive. There must be at least two special characters, which cannot be consecutive and must be separated by numbers. Given this information, which of the following would be a usable password?

A. 7*2!1l4r
B. jq@5m8$z
C. tb19^c6k
D. ad7?4*3z

0130. Which of the following numbers is *not* a prime number?

1, 2, 3, 5, 7, 11, 13, 17, 19

A. 13   **C.** 5
B. 1   **D.** 2

0131. Which of the following is a palindrome?

A. 682412286   **C.** 195484519
B. 321767123   **D.** 569383695

0132. In the diagram below, what would the address number be for house "A"?

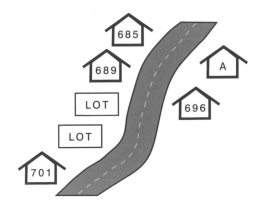

A. 688   **C.** 680
B. 692   **D.** 689

0133. Use the Coach to see the question sequence, then answer the question. [STOP] What were the letters in the order they appeared?

A. FTSR   **C.** HFSR
B. HFTR   **D.** HTFR

0134. Use the Coach to see the question sequence, then answer the question. [STOP] What were the letters in alphabetical order?

A. ABMP   **C.** ABOP
B. BMOP   **D.** AMOP

FIGURE 16

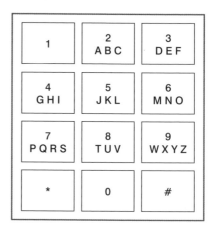

0135. Use the phone pad in Fig. 16 to decipher the word below.
Which letter is missing from the word?

74277_39

A. 3   **C.** 7
B. 6   **D.** 9

0136. Use the phone pad in Fig. 16 to decipher the word below.
Which letter is missing from the word?

_2736

A. 4   **C.** 9
B. 7   **D.** 5

0137. Use the phone pad in Fig. 16 to decipher the word below.
Which letter is missing from the word?

3732_

A. 6   **C.** 8
B. 4   **D.** 7

0138. Use the phone pad in Fig. 16 to decipher the word below.
Which letter is missing from the word?

34_25

A. 8   **C.** 4
B. 5   **D.** 6

0139. Use the phone pad in Fig. 16, how would you spell the following word in numbers? You must also determine what the missing letter is.

BARBE_UE

    A. 22723283   **C.** 22723583
    B. 2272783   **D.** 2272383

0140. Use the Coach to see the question sequence, then answer the question. [STOP] What was the fourth letter in the sequence?

    A. T   **C.** Q
    B. O   **D.** P

0141. Use the Coach to see the question sequence, then answer the question. [STOP] What word can be spelled using all of the letters?

    A. ROAM   **C.** FORD
    B. FROM   **D.** DORM

0142. Use the Coach to see the question sequence, then answer the question. [STOP] What was the fourth letter in the sequence?

    A. U   **C.** C
    B. O   **D.** Q

0143. Use the Coach to see the question sequence, then answer the question. [STOP] What were the letters in the order they appeared?

    A. RMTIL   **C.** RNTIL
    B. RMNTL   **D.** RMITL

0144. Use the Coach to see the question sequence, then answer the question. [STOP] What letter in the sequence came before the letter "F"?

    A. C   **C.** R
    B. D   **D.** O

0145. Use the Coach to see the question sequence, then answer the question. [STOP] How many vowels were in the sequence?

    A. Zero   **C.** Two
    B. One   **D.** Three

YAWNING INCREASES AWARENESS

Did you know that yawning actually increases your focus? Twenty percent of the oxygen we breathe is diverted to the brain, so yawning is like taking a quick shot of air. It's nature's way of saying, "stay alert."

FIGURE 17

Attention to detail is a critical skill set for a variety of profesions, including engineers, accountants, and investigators.

0146. Use the Coach to see the question sequence, then answer the question. [STOP] What was the middle letter in the sequence?

A.	H	**C.**	W
B.	X	**D.**	E

0147. Use the Coach to see the question sequence, then answer the question. [STOP] How many consonants were in the sequence?

A.	Four	**C.**	Two
B.	Three	**D.**	Five

0148. Count the number of the letter E's in Fig. 17 while reading the sentence. How many are there?

A.	Eight	**C.**	Nine
B.	Ten	**D.**	Seven

0149. Count the number of the letter T's in Fig. 17 while reading the sentence. How many are there?

A.	Ten	**C.**	Nine
B.	Eleven	**D.**	Twelve

0150. Read Fig. 17. Which word is misspelled?

A.	Engineers	**C.**	Attention
B.	Profesions	**D.**	Accountants

0151. How many times does the letter "I" directly precede the letter "M" in the bold sentences below?

Tim's impersonations of Mike are amazing imitations of Mike's immaculate image. I'm impressed by him and imagine you will be, too.

A.	Eight	**C.**	Nine
B.	Ten	**D.**	Seven

0152. How many times does the letter "A" directly precede the letter "N" in the bold sentence below?

An ant and an animal known as a newt announced that another anonymous animal planned to join the Alaskan artillery team.

   A. Nine   **C.** Eleven
   B. Twelve   **D.** Ten

0153. How many times does the letter "E" directly precede the letter "S" in the bold sentences below?

Trees are sometimes seen as necessary and essential aspects of nature because they supply oxygen so we can live. Sometimes trees are seen as aesthetic sites of serenity and sensational seasonal beauty. Trees are such a special natural essence.

   A. Thirteen   **C.** Seventeen
   B. Nine   **D.** Fourteen

0154. Press the on the Coach, then solve the equation as quickly as you can. The value of each letter corresponds to its placement in the alphabet, i.e. A=1, Z=26, etc.

T+C =

   A. 23   **C.** 22
   B. 21   **D.** 24

0155. Press the ⟳ on the Coach, then solve the equation as quickly as you can. The value of each letter corresponds to its placement in the alphabet, i.e. A=1, Z=26, etc.

G+Q =

   A. 24   **C.** 23
   B. 20   **D.** 22

0156. Press the ⟳ on the Coach, then solve the equation as quickly as you can. The value of each letter corresponds to its placement in the alphabet, i.e. A=1, Z=26, etc.

R+M-V =

   A. 9   **C.** 10
   B. 7   **D.** 8

EXECUTIVE

0146–
0156

LEGEND

◗ = A	♠ = E	■ = R	✿ = S
★ = T	◆ = N	▲ = L	♟ = I

0157. Press the ⏻ on the Coach, then answer the question as quickly as you can. Using the Legend, what symbols correspond to the following letters?

NRSL

A. ◆,■,✿,♟   C. ◆,■,★,▲
B. ◆,■,✿,◆   D. ◆,■,✿,▲

0158. Press the ⏻ on the Coach, then answer the question as quickly as you can. Using the Legend, what do the following symbols spell?

A. Saint   C. Taint
B. Sails   D. Santa

0159. Press the ⏻ on the Coach, then answer the question as quickly as you can. Using the Legend, what symbols correspond to the following letters?

LISTEN

A. ▲,♟,✿,★,▲,◆
B. ▲,♟,✿,★,▲,♠
C. ▲,♟,★,✿,♠,◆
D. ▲,♟,✿,★,♠,◆

0160. Press the ⏻ on the Coach, then answer the question as quickly as you can. Using the Legend, what symbols correspond to the following letters?

REAL

A. ■,▲,◗,▲   C. ■,♠,◗,♟
B. ■,♠,▲,♟   D. ■,♠,◗,▲

0161. Press the ⟳ on the Coach, then answer the question as quickly as you can. Using the Legend, what do the following symbols spell?

🐾 ▲ ◆ ★

A. Tent   **C.** Rent
B. Sent   **D.** Salt

0162. Use the Coach to see the question sequence, then answer the question. [STOP] What was the combination shown in alphabetical and numerical order, with letters first?

A. CL45   **C.** 15CL
B. LO15   **D.** CL15

0163. Use the Coach to see the question sequence, then answer the question. [STOP] What were the numbers shown in the combination in numerical order?

A. 09   **C.** 39
B. 89   **D.** 38

0164. Use the Coach to see the question sequence, then answer the question. [STOP] What were the letters shown in the combination in alphabetical order?

A. DP   **C.** DR
B. RP   **D.** PC

0165. Use the Coach to see the question sequence, then answer the question. [STOP] What was the combination shown in alphabetical and numerical order, with letters first?

A. 49CRS   **C.** CRS49
B. CPS49   **D.** CRP49

0166. Use the Coach to see the question sequence, then answer the question. [STOP] What was the sum of the numbers in the combination?

A. 8   **C.** 10
B. 9   **D.** 6

EXECUTIVE

0157–
0166

43

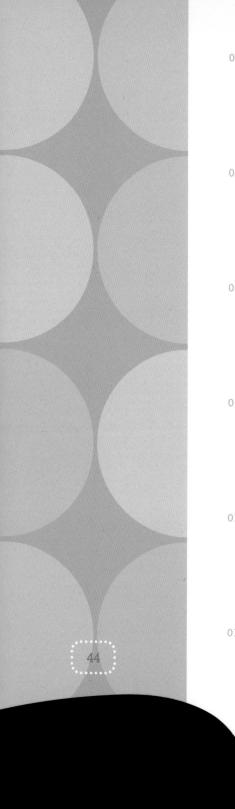

0167. Use the Coach to see the question sequence, then answer the question. [STOP] Which number did not appear in the combination?

A. 5   **C.** 2
B. 4   **D.** 9

0168. Use the Coach to see the question sequence, then answer the question. [STOP] Which number appeared twice in the combination?

A. 4   **C.** 8
B. 9   **D.** 3

0169. Use the Coach to see the question sequence, then answer the question. [STOP] What was the combination shown in alphabetical and numerical order, with letters first?

A. 348JRT   **C.** JRT348
B. JST238   **D.** JST348

0170. Use the Coach to see the question sequence, then answer the question. [STOP] What word did the letters in the combination spell?

A. CAST   **C.** CARP
B. CART   **D.** CASH

0171. Use the Coach to see the question sequence, then answer the question. [STOP] What were the letters in the combination in alphabetical order?

A. DKMR   **C.** DMR
B. DKM   **D.** DKMP

0172. How many times do consecutive numbers in the list tally to 15?

357893180931476435871394732875 4173

A. Five   **C.** Six
B. Four   **D.** Three

0173. What is the total if you add all of the numbers in the list?

3428743856731109473482734815276038

A. 147   C. 135
B. 151   D. 153

0174. Press the ↻ on the Coach, then study the diagram and answer the question as quickly as you can.

1 !!!
2 !!!
3 !!!
4 !!!
5 !!!
6 !!!

In which row is the only "I" located?

A. Row 3   C. Row 6
B. Row 5   D. Row 4

PURSE 1	PURSE 2	PURSE 3	PURSE 4
7 quarters	13 quarters	11 quarters	5 quarters
26 dimes	17 dimes	30 dimes	21 dimes
57 nickels	22 nickels	18 nickels	41 nickels
39 pennies	47 pennies	52 pennies	21 pennies
	1 silver dollar	1 fifty-cent piece	

0175. Which purse below has the most change?
A. Purse 4   C. Purse 3
B. Purse 2   D. Purse 1

0176. Decipher the answer using the bold sentences below.

Begin with the number of months in half a year.
Add a dozen doughnuts and a dozen eggs.
Multiply by the number of years in a decade.
Finally, add the number of minutes in an hour
plus the number of sides in a pentagon.

A. Always, always, yours
B. One year
C. Degrees in a circle
D. HD graphics card

BE PREPARED

You can increase the efficacy of your attention by mentally practicing the task prior to engaging in it. Just like an athlete or a musician rehearses an upcoming performance, you can take a moment and visualize yourself completing a task that lies ahead. So, before going any further in the program, stop and visualize yourself doing the next task. Imagine the room temperature, sounds around you, the brightness of the room, and the process of reading and responding to the Coach. By doing this, you will greatly enhance your attention and performance. If you find that you become distracted in the middle of a task, stop the task and use the same strategy to refocus. This strategy is typically called a "preparatory review."

0177. Figure out the relationship of the numbers within each box, then choose the missing number.

3	4
4	6

2	5
?	4

5	1
1	10

1	7
7	2

A. 2   **C.** 10
B. 4   **D.** 6

0178. How many times do consecutive numbers in the list tally to 12?

4873891893438765417384612874629874621947 43242

A. Five   **C.** Six
B. Seven   **D.** Eight

0179. Press the ↻ on the Coach, then study the diagram and answer the question as quickly as you can.

Which column contains the odd symbol?

A. Column 4   **C.** Column 3
B. Column 1   **D.** Column 2

0180. What is the sum total of the numbers in the list?

47389316248792618794126529918963872464

A. 185   **C.** 200
B. 197   **D.** 179

0181. You have five seconds to review the diagram. Press the ⏱ on the Coach, then answer the question as quickly as you can.

```
1  &&&&&&&&&&&&&&&&&&&&&&&&&&&&
2  &&&&&&&&&&&&&&&&&&&&&&&&&&&&
3  &&&&&&&&&&&&&&&&&&&&&&&&&&&&&
4  &&&&&&&&&&&&&&&&&&&&&&&$&&&&
5  &&&&&&&&&&&&&&&&&&&&&&&&&&&&
6  &&&&&&&&&&&&&&&&&&&&&&&&&&&&&
```

Which row contains the odd symbol?

    A. Row 4   **C.** Row 1

    B. Row 3   **D.** Row 5

0182. Which symbol appears only once in the list?

&$%$ ^ #$#**%$@&($#&(^%$%(!)&$##@#%^&**#$&)(#

    A. ?   **C.** !

    B.)   **D.** /

LEGEND

★ = E

0183. Solve the phrase below using the Legend above.

    A. The one I adore
    B. You are a smarty
    C. You are a friend
    D. You are a genius

0184. How many times do consecutive numbers in the list tally to 17?

326746783124981205861732460891742847148129

    A. Eight   **C.** Seven

    B. Five   **D.** Six

EXECUTIVE

0177–0184

47

0185. You have five seconds to review the diagram. Press the ⟳ on the Coach, then answer the question as quickly as you can.

1 ((
2 ((
3 ((
4 ((
5 ((
6 (((()((((((((((((((((((((((((((((((((((((((
7 ((

Which row contains the odd symbol?

A. Row 7   C. Row 6
B. Row 5   D. Row 3

0186. Figure out the relationship of the numbers within each box, then choose the missing number.

A. 3   C. 5
B. 2   D. 4

0187. You have five seconds to review the diagram. Press the ⟳ on the Coach, then answer the question as quickly as you can.

1 ♥♥♥♥♥♥♥♥♥♥♥♥♥♥♥♥♥
2 ♥♥♥♥♥♥♥♥♥♥♥♥♥♥♥♥♥
3 ♥♥♥♥♥♥♥♥♥♥♥♥♥♥♥♥♥
4 ♥♥♥♥♥♥♥♥♥♥♥♥♥♥♥♥♥
5 ♥♥♥♥♥♥♥♥♥♥♥♥♥♥♥♥♥
6 ♥♥♥♥♥♥♥♥♥♥♥♥♥♥♥♥♥
7 ♥♥♥♥♥♥♠♥♥♥♥♥♥♥♥♥
8 ♥♥♥♥♥♥♥♥♥♥♥♥♥♥♥♥♥
9 ♥♥♥♥♥♥♥♥♥♥♥♥♥♥♥♥♥

Which row contains the odd symbol?

A. Row 9   C. Row 7
B. Row 6   D. Row 8

FIGURE 18

Precious precocious pregnant puppies pretend to be princesses to prepare for the special puppy pageant.

0188. Which letter of the alphabet is missing from the list?

dfhdkdsbheiwjdkvjlkdtfiqhadjighemdnxiuxypzwqcr

A. O   **C.** Q
B. C   **D.** L

0189. Which letter of the alphabet appears most frequently in the list?

dfhdkdsbheiwjdkvjlkdtfiqhadjighemdnxiuxypzwqcr

A. D   **C.** Q
B. H   **D.** K

0190. You have five seconds to review the diagram. Press the ↻ on the Coach, then answer the question as quickly as you can.

1 . . . .
2 . . . .
3 . . . .
4 . . . .
5 . . . . , ...
6 . . . .
7 . . . .
8 . . . .

Which row above contains the odd symbol?

A. Row 5   **C.** Row 4
B. Row 6   **D.** No odd symbols

0191. How many P's are in Fig. 18?

A. Twelve   **C.** Fifteen
B. Eleven   **D.** Fourteen

0192. How many times does the letter "S" directly precede the letter "P" in Fig. 18?

A. Four   **C.** Five
B. Three   **D.** Two

EXECUTIVE

0185–0192

FIGURE 19

0193. How many items in Fig. 19 can hold or move liquid?

A. Six   **C.** Four
B. Five   **D.** Seven

0194. How many items in Fig. 19 can be associated with sound?

A. Six   **C.** Two
B. Three   **D.** Four

0195. Which event is represented in Fig. 19 by the most items?

    A. Christmas   **C.** Thanksgiving
    B. Wedding   **D.** Birthday

0196. How many items in Fig. 19 can be worn?

    A. Two   **C.** One
    B. None   **D.** Three

0197. Which item in Fig. 19 appears twice?

    A. Cake
    B. Bride and groom
    C. Bell
    D. Ink well

0198. Press the ⟳ on the Coach, then solve the equation as quickly as you can. The value of each letter corresponds to its placement in the alphabet, i.e. A=1, Z=26, etc.

$(J+R)/G =$

    A. B   **C.** D
    B. F   **D.** G

0199. Press the ⟳ on the Coach, then solve the equation as quickly as you can.The value of each letter corresponds to its placement in the alphabet, i.e. A=1, Z=26, etc., for this question.

$W+I =$

    A. 32   **C.** 33
    B. 34   **D.** 29

0200. Press the ⟳ on the Coach, then solve the equation as quickly as you can. The value of each letter corresponds to its placement in the alphabet, i.e. A=1, Z=26, etc., for this question.

$B+G =$

    A. 10   **C.** 9
    B. 7   **D.** 8

ORGANIZATION, PLANNING & LOGIC

Organization, Planning, and Logic are known as "higher order" brain functions. What this means is that these functions are dependent upon other, more elemental brain processes, such as effort, attention, concentration, speed of thinking, and memory.

Organization, specifically, is the placement of data in a logical sequence so as to make the future use of that data more efficient and effective. Planning is the formation of a definitive course of action or response to a specific situation or set of circumstances. And Logic can be defined as the rules that govern reasoning. Essentially, Organization, Planning, and Logic together represent the process of "thinking about your thinking."

"Higher order" functions, including Organization, Planning, and Logic, are physically located throughout the brain and utilize a vast set of neural networks that spans many regions and numerous depth levels. Because of this, the proper application of these higher order functions can enhance the brain's more elemental functions, such as attention, speed of mental processing, retention, and recall.

Picture yourself going to a tool shed to get a rake. You open the shed door, and the whole shed is piled with tools. There is such an enormous pile that it is at least three feet high and the whole width and depth of the shed. The rake is in there somewhere, but it will take some energy and effort to retrieve it. Now imagine that same shed meticulously organized. You open the door, and hanging right in front of you is the rake you want. As a matter of fact, there is not only the rake you want, but four other types of rakes to choose from. You make a mental note of where they are, and raking becomes just a little less tedious and draining.

With proper Organization, Planning, and Logic, the functions of the brain become streamlined, proficient, and successful. Proper preparation speeds up mental operations and protects against fatigue. Most importantly, Organization, Planning, and Logic is a skill set that can be learned and developed. So, with this chapter, let's begin clearing the cobwebs and organizing your mental tool shed!

FIGURE 1

DEPARTURE LOCATION

	First St. & First Ave.	Second St. & Second Ave.	Third St. & Third Ave.	Fourth St. & Fourth Ave.	Fifth St. & Fifth Ave.
7:00 a.m.	2537	5573	7357	3573	2573
7:30 a.m.	2573		5573		
7:45 a.m.			2537		3573
8:15 a.m.	3573		2573	5573	
8:30 a.m.		3573		2537	7357
9:00 a.m.	7357		3573	2573	5573
9:15 a.m.		7357			2537
10:00 a.m.	2537	5573	7357	3573	2573
10:30 a.m.			5573		
10:45 a.m.		2573	2537	7357	3573
11:15 a.m.	3573		2573	5573	
11:30 a.m.		3573		2537	7357
12:00 p.m.	7357		3573	2573	5573
Time from each departure location to the arrival location	5 minutes	10 minutes	15 minutes	20 minutes	25 minutes

NOTE: Bus routes are for Monday through Friday morning schedules and the arrival location is Main St. and First Ave. It takes five minutes to walk a block and two and a half minutes to sprint a block.

0201. Based on Fig. 1, which departure location has the most routes?

    A. Third St.   **C.** Fifth St.
    B. Fourth St.   **D.** First St.

0202. Based on Fig. 1, which departure location has the fewest routes?

    A. First St.   **C.** Second St.
    B. Fourth St.   **D.** Fifth St.

0203. Review Fig. 1. At the top of which hour(s) are there no bus stops?

    A. 8:00 a.m. and 11:00 a.m.
    B. 8:00 a.m.
    C. 11:00 a.m.
    D. 9:00 a.m. and 11:00 a.m.

0204. Based on Fig. 1, which bus has the most routes?

    A. Bus 5573   **C.** Bus 3573
    B. Bus 2537   **D.** Bus 2573

0205. Based on Fig. 1, which bus has the fewest routes?

    A. Bus 2573   **C.** Bus 2537
    B. Bus 7357   **D.** Bus 5573

0206. Review Fig. 1. What time will you arrive at First Ave. and Main St. if you take the earliest Bus 2573 departure from Third St.?

    A. 8:00 a.m.   **C.** 8:45 a.m.
    B. 8:30 a.m.   **D.** 11:30 a.m.

0207. Review Fig. 1. If you take the 10:00 a.m. Bus 2573, what time will you arrive at First Ave. and Main St.?

    A. 10:05 a.m.   **C.** 10:20 a.m.
    B. 10:10 a.m.   **D.** 10:25 a.m.

0208. Review Fig. 1 on p. 54. It's 11:15 a.m. and you are shopping at Breezey's Boutique, which is located at Second St. and Fifth Ave. Walking the shortest distance, which bus should you take to arrive at Main St. and First Ave. by 12:00 p.m., with the least amount of wait time at Main St. and First Ave.?

    A. 11:30 a.m. Bus 2573
    B. 12:00 p.m. Bus 7357
    C. 11:30 a.m. Bus 3573
    D. 11:30 a.m. Bus 7357

0209. Review Fig. 1 on p. 54. How long will it take you to get to Main St. if you start at Fourth St. and Second Ave. and walk to the 11:15 a.m. stop for Bus 3573?

    A. 30 minutes   **C.** 20 minutes
    B. 25 minutes   **D.** 35 minutes

0210. Review Fig. 1 on p. 54. You are at Third Ave. and Third St., and it is 10:30 a.m. What is the quickest way to get to Main St. and First Ave.?

    A. Sprint
    B. Walk
    C. Bus 5573 from that stop at 10:30 a.m.
    D. Walk to Second St., and take Bus 2573 at 10:45 a.m.

0211. Press the ↻ on the Coach, then answer the question as quickly as you can. What is the order of the cards from lowest to highest with aces high?

    A. 5 of hearts, 8 of clubs, 9 of diamonds, ace of spades
    B. Ace of spades, 5 of hearts, 8 of clubs, 9 of diamonds, jack of spades
    C. 5 of hearts, 9 of diamonds, jack of diamonds, ace of spades
    D. 5 of hearts, 8 of clubs, 9 of diamonds, jack of diamonds, ace of spades

FIGURE 2

TELEPHONE INFORMATION

Jane Smith 245-3326 Daytona, FL	Richard Black 242-9801 New York, NY	Sally Johnson 423-2311 Miami, FL	Amy Miles 312-3579 Boulder, CO
Mike Jones 655-9008 Dover, PA	Sara Tully 203-5664 Phoenix, AZ	Anne Carter 202-8745 Denver, CO	John Clay 789-3412 Millville, NJ
Sherry Parks 657-3391 Columbus, GA	Becky Barnes 221-3647 Orlando, FL	Scott Price 432-8511 Marion, SC	Julie Finn 321-6545 Orlando, FL
Carl Lam 434-9801 Camden, SC	Linda Jones 304-1552 Erie, PA	Ruth Mires 590-9762 Durham, NC	Tony Davis 319-6378 Dover, NJ

AREA CODES

MIAMI, FL	786	PHOENIX, AZ	520
BOULDER, CO	303	DOVER, PA	717
COLUMBUS, GA	706	DENVER, CO	720
ORLANDO, FL	407	MILLVILLE, NJ	856
CAMDEN, SC	803	DURHAM, NC	919
NEW YORK, NY	718	MARION, SC	843
DAYTONA, FL	386	ERIE, PA	814

0212. Based on Fig. 2, what is Ruth's area code?

    A. 386   **C.** 803
    B. 843   **D.** 919

0213. Based on Fig. 2, which city's area code is 856?

    A. Miami   **C.** Camden
    B. Daytona   **D.** Millville

0214. Review Fig. 2. Whose number is (843) 432-8511?

    A. Scott Price   **C.** Sherry Parks
    B. Sally Johnson   **D.** Jane Smith

0215. Most of the people listed in Fig. 2 live in which state?

    A. New Jersey   **C.** Colorado
    B. South Carolina   **D.** Florida

ORGANIZATION

0208–
0215

GETTING Zzzzs ...

Are you getting adequate, quality sleep? In order to function mentally and physically at their best, most adults require seven to eight hours of sleep nightly. The sleep must also pass through the five stages, known as Stages 1, 2, 3, 4, and REM (Rapid Eye Movement) Sleep. Approximately half of our sleep time is spent in Stage 2, 20 percent is spent in REM, and the remainder is split among the three other stages. Sleep influences our ability to be attentive, react quickly and appropriately, and create memories. Sleep also influences our general health, mood, and the body's ability to fight infection. It has also been established that people who get a good night's sleep typically do better when presented with mentally grueling tasks. So, if you want to improve your mental agility, don't compromise your sleep!

0216. Review Fig. 2 on p. 57. In which state do two people have the same last name?

    A. Colorado   **C.** New York
    B. Florida   **D.** Pennsylvania

0217. Based on Fig. 2 on p. 57, which two people share the same area code?

    A. Carl and Ruth   **C.** Amy and Anne
    B. Tony and Mike **D.** Julie and Becky

0218. Based on Fig. 2 on p. 57, which two people live in the same city but in different states?

    A. Becky and Julie
    B. Mike and Tony
    C. Jane and Sally
    D. John and Tony

0219. Based on Fig. 2 on p. 57, which of the following is in the correct numerical order (using area codes)?

    A. Phoenix, Daytona, Columbus, Miami
    B. Boulder, Denver, New York, Marion
    C. Boulder, Daytona, Orlando, Camden
    D. Orlando, Phoenix, Millville, Camden

0220. Based on Fig. 2 on p. 57, which of the following is in the correct alphabetical order using each person's last name?

    A. Erie, Phoenix, Daytona
    B. Miami, Denver, Boulder
    C. New York, Millville, Camden
    D. Durham, Camden, Boulder

0221. Review Fig. 2 on p. 57. Using the area codes, which two cities each have a sum of 13?

    A. Dover and Marion
    B. Columbus and Erie
    C. Columbus and Orlando
    D. Marion and Erie

FIGURE 3

LIBRARY CATEGORIES

HISTORY	EUH
MATH	TAM
SCIENCE	CIE
ENGLISH	EGL
TRAVEL	RVE

BOOKS CHECKED OUT

France, RVE006 (due back Nov. 14)
World War I, EUH004 (due back Nov. 24)
Introduction to Algebra I, TAM009 (due back Nov. 23)
Battle of the Bulge, EUH002 (due back Nov. 13)
Introduction to Geometry, TAM006 (due back Dec. 4)
Introduction to Neuroscience, CIE080 (due back Dec. 2)
Spelling and Punctuation, EGL075 (due Dec. 2)

0222. Based on Fig. 3, what category is *World War I* under?

    A. TAM   **C.** EUH
    B. CIE   **D.** RVE

0223. Review Fig. 3. Alphabetically, by book title, which of the books is third?

    A. RVE006   **C.** TAM009
    B. EUH004   **D.** TAM006

0224. Based on Fig. 3, how many books are due back in November?

    A. Three   **C.** Four
    B. Five   **D.** Two

0225. Based on Fig. 3, which two books are due back on the same day?

    A. *Intro to Neuroscience* and *Battle of the Bulge*
    B. *Geometry* and *Algebra 1*
    C. *Intro to Neuroscience* and *Spelling and Punctuation*
    D. *Advanced Neuroscience* and *Spelling and Punctuation*

0226. Based on Fig. 3, what is the title of TAM006?

    A. *Introduction to Algebra I*
    B. *Introduction to Geometry*
    C. *Introduction to Algebra II*
    D. *World War I*

0227. Based on Fig. 3, how many history books were checked out?

    A. Three   **C.** Five
    B. One   **D.** Two

0228. Based on Fig. 3, what category would the book titled *Medieval Times* be under?

    A. TAM   **C.** CIE
    B. EUH   **D.** RVE

0229. Based on Fig. 3, when is *Intro to Neuroscience* due back?

    A. Nov. 23   **C.** Dec. 2
    B. Nov. 13   **D.** Dec. 4

0230. Based on Fig. 3, what is the title of the book with the category number of EGL075?

    A. *World War I*   **C.** *Spelling*
    B. *English*   **D.** *Spelling and Punctuation*

0231. Based on Fig. 3, which book is due back first?

    A. RVE006   **C.** EUH002
    B. TAM006   **D.** CIE080

0232. Based on Fig. 3, which book is due back the last?

    A. TAM006   **C.** EUH004
    B. EGL075   **D.** CIE080

AWARENESS

It's very difficult to change a repeated behavior we are often unaware of. Frequently, cognitive decline or memory issues creep up on us subtly. So subtly, in fact, that even our closest loved ones may perceive this gradual pattern of behavior as normal, and not see any change. But it's important to know how your brain works as you get older. The diagnostic tool in this book is also useful in developing your awareness of brain areas that could use a "tune-up." Awareness of a deficit is the cornerstone of addressing the issue.

FIGURE 4

Apple	Lettuce	Spinach	*Carrot*
Corn	*Radish*	Lemon	*Beet*
Turnip	Venison	Orange	

0233. How many traditional fruits are included in Fig. 4?

    A. Nine   **C.** Seven
    B. Five   **D.** Six

0234. How many items included in Fig. 4 are normally yellow on the outside?

    A. Three   **C.** Two
    B. Four   **D.** Five

0235. What do the pictured items in Fig. 4 have in common?

    A. They are all grown on a vine
    B. They are all vegetables
    C. They are all fruits
    D. Their colors are all variations of the color red

0236. How many items in Fig. 4 have seeds?

    A. Nine
    B. Ten
    C. Eight
    D. Seven

0237. What do the foods listed in italics in Fig. 4 have in common?

    A. They are all the same color
    B. They are all tubers
    C. They are all root vegetables
    D. They are all the same shape

FIGURE 5

The Holiday Fund at the bank looks enticing. The bank is offering a non-interest-bearing account to collect your savings. You have five grown children, on whom you will spend $150 each, as well as on their spouses. Three of them are married. Two of your children have children of their own, for a total of three grandchildren, on whom you will spend $250 each.

0238. In which section of the grocery store would you find the majority of the items in Fig. 4?

    A. Frozen foods   **C.** Meats
    B. Deli   **D.** Produce

0239. Which item included in Fig. 4 is neither a fruit nor a vegetable?

    A. Tomato   **C.** Squash
    B. Venison   **D.** Eggplant

0240. Read Fig. 5. How much money will you need to save?

    A. $1,950   **C.** $1,500
    B. $1,250   **D.** $1,700

0241. Read Fig. 5. You have twenty-three pay periods to spread your savings. What is the minimum amount you need to save each pay period to reach your goal (rounded up by tens)?

    A. $70   **C.** $60
    B. $80   **D.** $90

0242. Read Fig. 5. The bank is offering a $5 bonus for each full month you maintain deposits of $1,000 or more in your Holiday Fund. There are two pay periods each month, including January and November. However, there are three pay periods in October. How much money will be in your account before you drain it on November 25 if you save $100 per pay period?

    A. $2,330   **C.** $2,230
    B. $2,300   **D.** $2,200

0243. How many vegetables are listed in Fig. 4?

    A. Eleven   **C.** Nine
    B. Seven   **D.** Ten

ORGANIZATION

0233–0243

FIGURE 6

TROOP MEETING SCHEDULE

GIRLS			BOYS		
Ruby*	Kindergarten & 1st grade	Tues. 7 p.m.	**Coal***	Kindergarten & 1st grade	Mon. 6 p.m.
Pearl	2nd & 3rd grade	Weds. 7 p.m.	**Shale***	2nd grade	Tues. 6 p.m.
Emerald	Ages 9–11 years	Thurs. 7 p.m.	**Pumice**	3rd grade	Weds. 6 p.m.
Sapphire	Ages 11–16 years	Weds. 8 p.m.	**Quartz**	4th & 5th grade	Thurs. 6 p.m.
			Granite	Ages 11–16	Tues. 8 p.m.

* Meets biweekly

TROOP MEMBERS

Brown, Sandra	2nd	Brady, Lily	1st	Johnson, Kevin	15
Smith, Michael	11	Johns, Todd	4th	Freeman, Cindy	9
Johnson, Kimberly	13	Thomas, Linda	15	Rose, Travis	3rd
Carlson, Ron	12	Long, Tina	10	Waters, Derek	2nd
Martin, Misty	3rd	Norton, Jill	12	Jones, Marcus	2nd
Parker, Thomas	3rd	**Johnson, Mary**	3rd	**Davis, Katie**	3rd
Franks, Trevor	4th	Mills, Angela	K	Hudson, Bart	3rd
Wilson, Marcia	10	Gase, Amanda	1st	Land, Jason	2nd
Owens, John	5th	Nixon, Lisa	16	Simpson, Drake	3rd
Munns, Robert	4th	Adams, Rose	2nd	Turner, Sara	10
Evans, Gina	K	Pratt, Duncan	15	**Hill, Mandi**	3rd

0244. Based on Fig. 6, which grade level has the greatest participation?

    A. Third   **C.** Fourth

    B. Second   **D.** First

0245. Based on Fig. 6, how many Quartz need to be recruited to have half a dozen participants?

    A. None   **C.** One

    B. Three   **D.** Two

0246. Based on Fig. 6, which troop has the most members?

    A. Pearl   **C.** Pumice
    B. Quartz   **D.** Emerald

0247. Review Fig. 6. The boys' troop needs an additional one-hour meeting to prepare for a camping trip. All troops meet at the same location, and the venue will not allow any new time slots or extended hours. What is their best option?

    A. Meet during the Coal group's meeting time
    B. Meet at 7 p.m. during the week the Ruby group is off
    C. Meet at 6 p.m. during the week the Shale group is off
    D. Find another meeting spot

0248. Review Fig. 6. Anita Jones is a second-grader. Which troop is she eligible to join?

    A. Ruby   **C.** Shale
    B. Coal   **D.** Pearl

0249. Based on Fig. 6, which time slot is available weekly for extra meetings?

    A. Every other Tuesday at 6 p.m.
    B. Every other Tuesday at 7 p.m.
    C. Every Monday at 6 p.m.
    D. No time slots are available

0250. Based on Fig. 6, how many more girls than boys participate?

    A. One   **C.** Two
    B. Three   **D.** Five

0251. Study Fig. 6. What does the boldface type in the Troop Members chart denote?

    A. Third-grade girls
    B. Children who will be moving from grade-level grouping to the general age-level grouping
    C. Group leaders
    D. Third-grade boys

0252. Review Fig. 6 on p. 64. All the troops have agreed to reduce the room reservations by four hours each month, Tuesday through Friday. What is the most efficient way to reorganize the meeting schedule?

   A. Change the Shale meeting to biweekly on Tuesdays at 7 p.m.
   B. Change the Ruby meeting to biweekly on Tuesdays at 6 p.m.
   C. Combine the Shale and Pumice meetings
   D. Combine the Pearl and Sapphire meetings on Thursdays

0253. Review Fig. 6 on p. 64. Alphabetically, by last name, who is the third child in the Pearl troop?

   A. Brown, Sandra
   B. Johnson, Mary
   C. Davis, Katie
   D. Rose, Travis

0254. Based on Fig. 6 on p. 64, which of the Johnson children is the youngest?

   A. Mary   **C.** Marcus
   B. Kimberly   **D.** Todd

0255. Based on Fig. 6 on p. 64, how many second- and third-grade children are involved?

   A. Ten   **C.** Seven
   B. Six   **D.** Thirteen

0256. Review Fig. 6 on p. 64. Eleven-year-old Theresa King wants to join the troop. She has never been involved in a club of this nature before and is in the fifth grade. In which troop should she be placed?

   A. Quartz   **C.** Sapphire
   B. Emerald   **D.** Granite

FIGURE 7

$^1/_2$ lb, 16 oz, 4.2 oz, 2 lbs, 7.2 oz, $^1/_4$ lb, $2^1/_2$ lbs, 1 lb 6 oz, $^1/_3$ lb

0257. Review Fig. 6 on p. 64. A joint activity is being organized including these groups: Ruby, Pearl, Coal, Shale, Pumice, and Quartz. In general, the leaders plan for one adult to every three children in Kindergarten–2nd grade, and one adult to every five children in 3rd–5th grade. How many adults are needed at minimum if all children participate?

    A. Six   **C.** Seven
    B. Five   **D.** Four

0258. Review Fig. 6 on p. 64. Who is the oldest child participating?

    A. Lisa Nixon
    B. Kevin Johnson
    C. Duncan Pratt
    D. Linda Thomas

0259. Boxes of chocolates come in the sizes listed in Fig. 7. What is the smallest box of chocolates available?

    A. $^1/_4$ lb   **C.** $^1/_3$ lb
    B. 4.2 oz   **D.** $^1/_2$ lb

0260. Boxes of chocolates come in the sizes listed in Fig. 7. How many ounces are in the largest box of chocolates available?

    A. 3.6 oz   **C.** 22 oz
    B. 40 oz   **D.** 48 oz

0261. The U.S. post office initially sorts mail by what category?

    A. Zip code   **C.** Street address
    B. Size   **D.** Name

0262. You just dropped your toolbox. What is the order of the nut sizes below, from smallest to largest?

    $^3/_4$, $^3/_8$, $^7/_{32}$, $^7/_{16}$, $^{55}/_{64}$

    A. $^7/_{32}$, $^3/_8$, $^7/_{16}$, $^{55}/_{64}$, $^3/_4$
    B. $^3/_8$, $^7/_{32}$, $^7/_{16}$, $^3/_4$, $^{55}/_{64}$
    C. $^7/_{32}$, $^3/_8$, $^7/_{16}$, $^3/_4$, $^{55}/_{64}$
    D. $^3/_8$, $^7/_{16}$, $^7/_{32}$, $^3/_4$, $^{55}/_{64}$

TECH TOOLS

Let technology be your friend as you develop Organization and Planning strategies. We are accessorized with a variety of technological tools designed to make life more manageable and to reduce the amount of information our brain must remember. Cell phones allow us to store important phone numbers, set alarms as reminders, and some even allow us to manage our e-mail and calendars. If this works for you, remember to use the tools faithfully. Some people prefer to e-mail and use the calendar on their computer. Again, if you select that option, use it faithfully. Paper calendars continue to serve as an effective means of organizing your life. Just remember that, whichever means you choose, it needs to work for you, and you must use it loyally and solely. If you start mixing your means of organization—some things on e-mail, some on the phone, others on paper, you are sure to double-book yourself or overlook an important appointment or event. Again, choose the means of organization with which you are most comfortable, and then use it exclusively so that it is a reliable source of information. Now your mind is free to focus on other engaging tasks more efficiently.

FIGURE 8

Turtle	Dolphin	Crocodile
Clown Fish	Bullfrog	Newt
Lizard	Giraffe	Hippopotamus
Rhinoceros	Salamander	Snake

0263. Which of the following answer choices correctly alphabetizes the amphibians in Fig. 8?

    A. Bullfrog, Newt, Salamander
    B. Bullfrog, Clown Fish, Crocodile, Dolphin
    C. Bullfrog, Clown Fish, Newt, Salamander
    D. Bullfrog, Crocodile, Dolphin, Turtle

0264. One of the animals listed in Fig. 8 is the only one of a scientific class; all other animals have at least one other animal within the same class. Which animal is in a scientific class alone?

    A. Clown Fish   **C.** Lizard
    B. Dolphin   **D.** Newt

0265. Which scientific classification does the dolphin belong to?

    A. Amphibians   **C.** Mammals
    B. Fish   **D.** Reptiles

0266. How many animals listed in Fig. 8 can be the color green?

    A. Four   **C.** Five
    B. Six   **D.** Seven

0267. How many reptiles are listed in Fig. 8?

    A. Four   **C.** One
    B. Three   **D.** Two

0268. How many mammals are listed in Fig. 8?

    A. Four   **C.** Two
    B. Five   **D.** Three

ORGANIZATION

0263–
0268

FIGURE 9

TOP 15 MLB HOME RUN HITTERS

PLAYER	TEAM	RBI'S	HOME RUNS
Barry Bonds	San Francisco Giants	1,996	762
Reggie Jackson	Oakland Athletics	1,702	563
Babe Ruth	New York Yankees	2,217	714
Sammy Sosa	Baltimore Orioles	1,667	609
Harmon Killebrew	Kansas City Royals	1,584	573
Frank Robinson	Cleveland Indians	1,812	586
Alex Rodriguez	New York Yankees	1,606	553
Mike Schmidt	Philadelphia Phillies	1,595	548
Hank Aaron	Milwaukee Brewers	2,297	755
Jim Thome	Chicago White Sox	1,488	541
Willie Mays	New York Mets	1,903	660
Mickey Mantle	New York Yankees	1,509	536
Mark McGwire	St. Louis Cardinals	1,414	583
Ken Griffey Jr.	Chicago White Sox	1,772	611
Rafael Palmeiro	Baltimore Orioles	1,835	569

Source: www.mlb.com

0269. Based on Fig. 9, which player hit the most home runs?

A. Willie Mays   **C.** Barry Bonds
B. Hank Aaron   **D.** Babe Ruth

0270. Based on Fig. 9, which player has the least RBI's?

A. Hank Aaron   **C.** Mickey Mantle
B. Jim Thome   **D.** Mark McGwire

0271. Based on Fig. 9, what is the total number of home runs hit by all players?

A. 9,636   **C.** 9,031
B. 9,631   **D.** 9,163

0272. Based on Fig. 9, which team had the most home run hitters?

A. Chicago White Sox
B. New York Yankees
C. Baltimore Orioles
D. Cleveland Indians

0273. Based on Fig. 9, which of the following players had the most RBI's and home runs?

    A. Harmon Killebrew
    B. Reggie Jackson
    C. Sammy Sosa
    D. Mike Schmidt

0274. Based on Fig. 9, which two players were closest in the amount of home runs they hit?

    A. Schmidt and Thome
    B. Robinson and McGwire
    C. Palmeiro and Jackson
    D. Griffey Jr. and Sosa

0275. Based on Fig. 9, what is the total number of RBI's for the New York Yankees?

    A. 6,914   **C.** 7,235
    B. 1,803   **D.** 5,332

0276. Based on Fig. 9, which player's RBI's and home runs total 2,398?

    A. Griffey Jr.   **C.** Robinson
    B. Sosa   **D.** Thome

0277. Based on Fig. 9, which teams are listed below in numerical order using total RBI's?

    A. Chicago White Sox, Baltimore Orioles, New York Yankees
    B. Chicago White Sox, New York Yankees, Baltimore Orioles
    C. San Francisco Giants, Milwaukee Brewers, Philadelphia Phillies
    D. Kansas City Royals, St. Louis Cardinals, Oakland Athletics

0278. Based on Fig. 9, which players are listed below in reverse numerical order using home runs?

    A. Bonds, McGwire, Ruth
    B. Ruth, Mays, Aaron
    C. Robinson, Sosa, Killebrew
    D. Jackson, Rodriguez, Schmidt

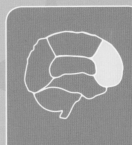

FIGURE 10

MAXIMIZE WITH MENTAL MATH

To really exercise your brain when using this program and during day-to-day activities, such as calculating groceries, monthly bills, and restaurant tips, you should try to do the math in your head instead of using a cal- culator. You may have to work the problem more than once, but it will benefit your brain span more to do mental math versus exercising your fingers on a calculator.

Your boss has instructed you to arrange a cocktail party for the staff of 75 people, allowing each employee 1 guest. You are responsible for maintaining the budget and ensuring sufficient food is prepared.

Jumbo Shrimp, 16–20 shrimp per pound	$21.95
Buffalo Wings, 60 count	$25.49
Cheese Trays, 30 servings	$65.00
Fresh Fruit, 25 servings	$52.50
Water, case of 24	$15.50
Diet Soda, case of 24	$16.00
Soda, case of 24	$15.75
Juice, case of 24	$21.25

0279. Review Fig. 10. Assuming full attendance, how much shrimp should you order following the allowance guideline of 3 shrimp per guest?

    A. 29 pounds   **C.** 15 pounds
    B. 23 pounds   **D.** 25 pounds

0280. Review Fig. 10. You decide to purchase cheese and fruit trays to feed 150 guests. What will the cost be for these trays?

    A. $640.00   **C.** $587.50
    B. $117.50   **D.** $705.00

0281. Review Fig. 10. You expect 85 percent of the staff will attend, and 65 percent of those attending will bring a guest. How many guests should you plan for? Round up to whole numbers.

    A. 113   **C.** 211
    B. 104   **D.** 106

0282. Review Fig. 10. The catering company advises that 50 per- cent of the guests will drink 1 bottle of water and 1 soda, 10 percent of the guests will drink 1 juice and 1 water, 10 percent will consume a single water, and 30 percent will drink 2 sodas. Of the soda drinkers, 25 percent will opt for a diet soda. Note that packages cannot be broken, and you do not want a shortage. What is the total cost of beverages for full attendance?

    A. $209.00   **C.** $225.25
    B. $194.00   **D.** $210.75

0283. Review Fig. 10. The catering company has an abundance of chicken wings and has offered you a 15 percent discount if you order 300 wings. What would the total cost of wings be?

A. $127.45
B. $108.33
C. $19.11
D. $130.00

0284. Review Fig. 10. The catering company recommends the following: 30 pounds of shrimp, 300 chicken wings, 5 cheese trays, 6 fruit trays, 6 cases of water, 3 cases of diet soda, 5 cases of soda, and 2 cases of juice. The room rental for the event is a flat fee of $500. Your boss allowed you to spend $15 per person for 150 people. How much are you over or under your budget?

A. $88.81 under
B. $61.80 over
C. $61.80 under
D. $561.80 under

0285. Review Fig. 10. You negotiated a 10 percent discount on shrimp and wings and a 5 percent discount on cheese and fruit trays. What is the discount in dollars you will receive if you order 7 pounds of shrimp, 240 wings, 4 cheese trays, and 5 fruit trays?

A. $38.91
B. $77.81
C. $51.69
D. $65.03

0286. Review Fig. 10. If you expect 150 guests, how many trays of fruit should you order for each person to have one serving?

A. 3
B. 5
C. 1
D. 6

0287. Review Fig. 10. If you allow 4 wings per person, how many wings should you order, assuming full attendance, including employees' guests?

A. 300
B. 10
C. 600
D. 500

0288. Review Fig. 10. For conservative planning purposes, how many shrimp per pound should you estimate are included in each pound you order?

A. 20
B. 18
C. 16
D. 19

FIGURE 11

ADMISSION:
Matinee (before 3:00 p.m.) $5.50
Child Admission (under 10 years) $5.00
Adult Admission $8.00
Senior Admission (over 55 years) $6.50
Student Admission $6.50

SHOWTIMES:
Luna (PG) (122 min.) ***
11:00, 12:10, 3:00, 4:10, 6:00
Crash and Burn (R) (95 min.) **
5:00, 5:35, 6:00, 6:35, 7:00, 7:35
The Little Dragon (PG) (101 min.) **
11:15, 12:15, 2:15, 3:15, 5:15, 6:15
Complexity (R) (100 min.) ****
3:30, 4:00, 6:30, 8:00, 9:30, 10:00, 11:30
Have Faith (PG-13) (120 min.) ***
1:10, 3:10, 5:10, 7:10, 9:10
Whiskers (PG) (90 min.) ****
12:00, 12:50, 1:40, 2:30, 3:20, 4:10, 5:50, 6:40
Into the Silence (R) (110 min.) ***
4:45, 6:00, 7:15, 8:30, 9:45, 11:00
The Fallen (R) (93 min.) **
5:15, 7:00, 9:15, 11:00
Good Luck Sally (PG-13) (98 min.) ****
2:20, 3:10, 4:00, 5:15, 6:45, 8:00, 9:20
My Story (PG-13) (105 min.) ***
3:00, 4:45, 6:00, 7:15, 9:30, 10:10

0289. Based on Fig. 11, which movie has the most show times?

    A. *Complexity*   **C.** *Good Luck Sally*
    B. *Whiskers*   **D.** *The Little Dragon*

0290. Based on Fig. 11, which movie runs for 1 hour and 45 minutes?

    A. *The Fallen*   **C.** *My Story*
    B. *Whiskers*   **D.** *Complexity*

0291. Based on Fig. 11, which of the following movies are listed in correct numerical order according to running time?

    A. *The Fallen, My Story, Whiskers*
    B. *Complexity, Into the Silence, Luna*
    C. *Crash and Burn, Have Faith, Complexity*
    D. *Whiskers, Into the Silence, The Fallen*

0292. Based on Fig. 11, how much would it cost 2 adults to see *Good Luck Sally* at 2:20 p.m.?

  A. $11.50   **C.** $13.00
  B. $16.00   **D.** $11.00

0293. Based on Fig. 11, how much would it cost a fifty-seven-year-old female to see every showing of *Have Faith*?

  A. $31.50   **C.** $35.00
  B. $32.50   **D.** $38.00

0294. Based on Fig. 11, if you went to see *The Fallen* at 9:15, what time would the movie be over?

  A. 10:33   **C.** 11:08
  B. 10:48   **D.** 10:38

0295. Based on Fig. 11, if you only had 1 hour and 35 minutes to watch a movie, which of the following could you see (and be able to watch the entire film)?

  A. *Complexity*   **C.** *The Fallen*
  B. *Good Luck Sally* **D.** *The Little Dragon*

0296. Based on Fig. 11, how long would it take to watch one showing of each movie?

  A. 17 hr., 23 min.   **C.** 17 hr., 14 min.
  B. 15 hr., 33 min.   **D.** 17 hr., 40 min.

0297. Based on Fig. 11, if you had dinner reservations at 7:30 and expected the meal to take 1.25 hours, and you needed to drive 30 minutes to the theater, which movie would you arrive just in time to see?

  A. *The Fallen*   **C.** *Into the Silence*
  B. *Have Faith*   **D.** *Complexity or My Story*

0298. Based on Fig. 11, if you went to see *Have Faith* at 5:10 and then immediately went to see *My Story*, what time would you leave the theater?

  A. 8:45   **C.** 9:15
  B. 9:00   **D.** 9:30

NEED FOR SPEED

There is a growing body of research that clearly demonstrates that cognitive processing speed may be the most important aspect to consider when looking at age-related changes in cognition. The premise of neurocognitive rehabilitation is to intensively and regularly challenge your cognitive abilities, thereby improving the speed at which you are able to accurately move large amounts of data.

FIGURE 12

NUTRITION FACTS

FOOD	FAT (grams)	CAL.	PROTEIN (grams)	FOOD	FAT (grams)	CAL.	PROTEIN (grams)
8 oz Black Coffee	0	2	0	Ham and Cheese Sandwich	15	352	21
8 oz Orange Juice	0	110	1	3 oz Pork Chop	13	205	21
1 cup Whole Milk	8	150	8	8 oz Sirloin Steak	8	160	46
1 Scrambled Egg	12	160	12	Grilled Chicken Caesar Salad w/ Dressing	27	380	26
1 cup Corn Flakes	0	101	2	Fettuccini Alfredo	16	370	14
English Muffin w/ Butter	6	189	5	Chicken Noodle Soup	3	120	8
2 Slices of Bacon	2	27	3	Grilled Cheese Sandwich	27	420	16
1 Banana	0	105	1	Steamed Broccoli	0	25	2
Blueberry Cereal Bar	3	110	3	Steamed Corn	1	80	3
Pretzels	1	110	2	Steamed Green Beans	0	20	1
Tortilla Chips	11	219	3	Baked Potato w/ Butter and Sour Cream	24	495	8
Corn Chips	10	160	2	Rice Pilaf	1	190	4
Potato Chips	10	152	2	Rice Pudding	4	140	4
Salsa	0	10	0	Chocolate Raisins	6	170	2
Plain Yogurt	3	150	13	Coffee Cake	5	140	2
Banana Nut Muffin	7	150	2	Glazed Donut	12	250	4
Peanut Butter Crackers (6)	10	193	4	Vanilla Ice Cream	7	130	2
Peanut Butter and Jelly Sandwich	14	343	10	Diet Cola	0	0	0
Cola	0	110	0	Sweet Iced Tea	0	70	0
Glass White Wine	0	70	0	Glass Red Wine	0	84	0

Source: www.peertrainer.com

DAILY FOOD LOG

	MONDAY	TUESDAY	WEDNESDAY	THURSDAY	FRIDAY
Breakfast	1 Scrambled Egg, 2 Slices of Bacon, Black Coffee	Banana, Black Coffee	Bowl of Corn Flakes w/ 1 cup Whole Milk	Black Coffee	English Muffin w/ Butter, 8 oz Orange Juice
Snack	Pretzels, Diet Cola	Blueberry Cereal Bar, Black Coffee		Banana Nut Muffin, Black Coffee	Peanut Butter Crackers (6), Cola
Lunch	Peanut Butter and Jelly Sandwich, Potato Chips, Water	Ham and Cheese Sandwich, Corn Chips, Diet Cola	Grilled Cheese Sandwich, Banana, Water	Chicken Caesar Salad w/ Dressing, Sweet Iced Tea	
Snack	Glazed Donut, Black Coffee	Pretzels, Diet Cola		Tortilla Chips w/ Salsa, Water	Plain Yogurt, Banana, Black Coffee
Dinner	8 oz Grilled Sirloin Steak, Baked Potato w/ Butter and Sour Cream, Steamed Corn, Glass of Red Wine	2–6 oz Grilled Pork Chops, Rice Pilaf, Steamed Green Beans, Diet Cola	Fettuccini Alfredo, Steamed Broccoli, Glass of White Wine		Chicken Noodle Soup, Grilled Cheese Sandwich, Black Coffee
Snack	Chocolate Covered Raisins		Rice Pudding	Coffee Cake, Black Coffee	Vanilla Ice Cream

0299. Review the charts in Fig. 12. On which day were the most calories consumed during breakfast?

A. Friday   **C.** Monday

B. Tuesday   **D.** Wednesday

0300. Review the charts in Fig. 12. How many combined grams of fat and protein does a Ham and Cheese Sandwich have?

A. 21 grams   **C.** 15 grams

B. 352 grams   **D.** 36 grams

0301. Review the charts in Fig. 12. How many calories were consumed for lunch on Tuesday?

A. 571 calories   **C.** 522 calories

B. 512 calories   **D.** 521 calories

0302. Review the charts in Fig. 12. On which day were the most grams of protein consumed during lunch?

A. Tuesday   **C.** Thursday

B. Wednesday   **D.** Monday

0303. Review the charts in Fig. 12 on pgs. 76–77. How many grams of fat were consumed for breakfast during the week?

    A. 32 grams   **C.** 14 grams
    B. 28 grams   **D.** 49 grams

0304. Review the charts in Fig. 12 on pgs. 76–77. On which day was the least amount of fat consumed during lunch?

    A. Monday   **C.** Wednesday
    B. Tuesday   **D.** Thursday

0305. Review the charts in Fig. 12 on pgs. 76–77. Which snack, including the beverage, has the least amount of fat?

    A. Tortilla Chips w/ Salsa and Water
    B. Blueberry Cereal Bar and Black Coffee
    C. Peanut Butter Crackers and Cola
    D. Pretzels and Diet Cola

0306. Review the charts in Fig. 12 on pgs. 76–77. On Wednesday, which snack could be added to total 10 grams of fat and 230 calories?

    A. Banana and Plain Yogurt
    B. Coffee Cake and Black Coffee
    C. Corn Chips and Sweet Tea
    D. Potato Chips and Diet Cola

0307. Review the charts in Fig. 12 on pgs. 76–77. Which of the following lists is in correct numerical order according to fat grams?

    A. Banana, Pretzels, Rice Pudding, Vanilla Ice Cream
    B. Plain Yogurt, Corn Chips, Coffee Cake
    C. Black Coffee, Vanilla Ice Cream, Rice Pudding
    D. Orange Juice, Tortilla Chips, Chocolate Raisins

0308. Review the charts in Fig. 12 on pgs. 76–77. Which of the following morning snacks would keep Wednesday's calories under 1,535?

    A. Corn Chips and Sweet Tea
    B. Banana Nut Muffin and Coffee
    C. Plain Yogurt and Banana
    D. Pretzels and Sweet Iced Tea

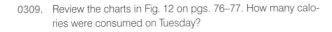

0309. Review the charts in Fig. 12 on pgs. 76–77. How many calories were consumed on Tuesday?

    A. 1,651 calories   **C.** 1,598 calories
    B. 1,461 calories   **D.** 1,871 calories

0310. Review the charts in Fig. 12 on pgs. 76–77. On which day was the most protein consumed?

    A. Tuesday   **C.** Wednesday
    B. Monday   **D.** Friday

0311. Review the charts in Fig. 12 on pgs. 76–77. Which of the following lists includes the days of the week in order based on the calorie intake from greatest to least?

    A. Tuesday, Wednesday, Friday, Monday
    B. Monday, Tuesday, Friday, Wednesday, Thursday
    C. Tuesday, Friday, Wednesday, Thursday, Monday
    D. Monday, Tuesday, Wednesday, Friday, Thursday

0312. Review the charts in Fig. 12 on pgs. 76–77. Which entrée offers the most protein?

    A. Grilled Cheese Sandwich
    B. 6 oz Pork Chop
    C. 3 oz Pork Chop
    D. 8 oz Sirloin Steak

0313. Review the charts in Fig. 12 on pgs. 76–77. Which beverage has the most calories?

    A. Orange Juice   **C.** Cola
    B. Whole Milk   **D.** Red Wine

0314. How are clothing racks in stores generally first sorted?

    A. By gender   **C.** By color
    B. By size   **D.** By style

0315. Money is usually sorted by what category?

    A. Denomination   **C.** Color
    B. Face   **D.** Date

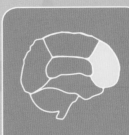

FIGURE 13

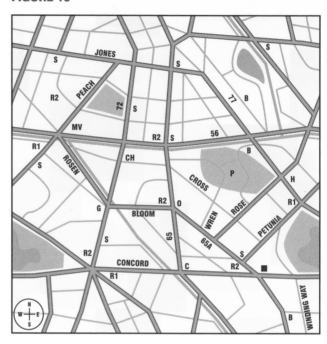

LEGEND

|⊢———⊣| **¹/₂ INCH = 2 MILES**

■ = Home
B = Bank
C = Church
CH = Courthouse
G = Gym; open 6 a.m.–midnight
H = Hospital
MV = Motor Vehicles; open 7:30 a.m.–
    4:30 p.m. M, T, TH, F
O = Office; work hours 9 a.m.–5 p.m.
P = City park
R1 = Sit-down restaurant
R2 = Fast-food restaurant
S = Supermarket; open 8 a.m.–10 p.m.
■ to O = 15 min.
■ to G = 25 min.
G to O = 15 min.
■ to C = 15 min.
■ to MV = 45 min.
G to MV = 20 min.
MV to O = 30 min.
Routine time at G = 6:30 a.m.–7:30 a.m.

NOTE: It's Monday, and it promises to be a busy day. You absolutely must go to the motor vehicle office because your tags are expired. It will take at least an hour to get your tags there.

0316. Review Fig. 13. Arrange your day. How will you do it all?

    A. Call in sick
    B. Cut down gym time down by 15 minutes
    C. Go to the gym 20 minutes earlier
    D. Go to the motor vehicle office after work

0317. Review Fig. 13. You normally take route 65A to work. However, there has been an accident, and you want to avoid 65A at 65A and Rose. What is the best alternate route?

    A. Left on Concord, left on Winding Way, left on Petunia, right on Cross, and left on Wren
    B. Left on Concord to 65A, right on Petunia, left on Cross, and left on Wren
    C. Right on Concord, right on 65, right on 65A, and left on Wren
    D. Right on Concord, right on 65, right on Cross, right on Wren

0318. Review Fig. 13. Approximately how far is it from home to the office?

    A. 15 miles   **C.** 6 miles
    B. 4 miles   **D.** 5 miles

0319. Review Fig. 13. Which routes intersect in front of the courthouse?

    A. 65 and 72   **C.** Rosen and 72
    B. 56 and 72   **D.** 56 and 65

0320. Review Fig. 13. Which road has the sit-down restaurant nearest to your home?

    A. Peach   **C.** 65A
    B. Concord   **D.** Petunia

0321. Review Fig. 13 on p. 80. You forgot to make brownies to take to the church potluck. The potluck starts at 6:15 p.m. The brownies take 10 minutes to prepare and 30 minutes to bake. What time do you need to leave work in order to make it home to mix and bake the brownies?

    A. 5:15 p.m.   **C.** 4:30 p.m.
    B. 5:30 p.m.   **D.** 5:05 p.m.

0322. Review Fig. 13 on p. 80. In what direction would you travel to get from the hospital to the courthouse?

    A. NE   **C.** NW
    B. Left   **D.** SE

0323. Review Fig. 13 on p. 80. What is the best route from home to work by making the fewest right turns and no left turns? There is no access to the office lot from 65A.

    A. Right on Concord, right on 65, right on Cross, right on Wren, right to office lot
    B. Right on Concord, right on 72, right on 56, right on 77, right on Rose, right on 65A, right to office lot
    C. Right on Concord, right on 65A, right on 65, right on Cross, right on Wren, right to office lot
    D. Right on Concord, right on 65A, right to office lot

0324. Review Fig. 13 on p. 80. What is the best route from the gym to the bank by making the fewest and most efficient turns?

    A. Northeast 72 to East 56
    B. East Broom to North 65 to East 56
    C. Northwest Rosen to East 56
    D. Southwest 72, East Concord, North 65, East 56

0325. Review Fig. 13 on p. 80. How many supermarkets are located in your area?

    A. Five   **C.** Six
    B. Eight   **D.** Seven

FIGURE 14

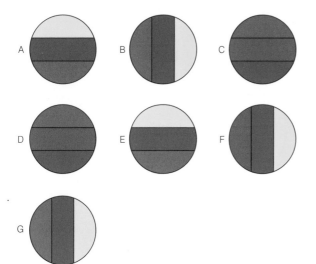

0326. In Fig. 14, which ball matches B?

    A. F   **C.** G
    B. A   **D.** C

0327. In Fig. 14, which ball does *not* have a match?

    A. C   **C.** F
    B. A   **D.** G

0328. In Fig. 14, how many balls have vertical stripes?

    A. Two   **C.** One
    B. Three   **D.** Four

0329. In Fig. 14, which ball matches C?

    A. B   **C.** A
    B. E   **D.** D

0330. Schools typically divide children by what category?

    A. Age   **C.** Height
    B. Grade   **D.** Weight

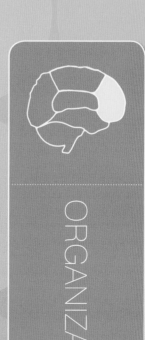

TOO EASY?

Try this! If you want to increase the difficulty of any task set forth in this book, add a distraction while working through the problems. For instance, you might want to tap your left foot for odd number questions and tap your right foot for even number questions. You could snap your fingers every time you encounter the word "the" and clap your hands for the word "and." This type of multitasking further challenges your brain, improving your overall brain span.

FIGURE 15

FLIGHT SCHEDULES

COMPANY	FLIGHT #	DEPART	ARRIVE	STOPS	TIME	PRICE
Tribute Air	T598	MCO	LAX	1- DFW	8 hr 31 min	$289.00
Morning Star	2965	MIA	SAN	1-IAH	9 hr 22 min	$301.00
Value Air	3475	TPA	SAN	2-DFW, LAX	11 hr 41 min	$299.00
Tribute Air	T349	TPA	SAN	1-MEM	8 hr 51 min	$277.00
Safety Express	21A5	MCO	LAX	1-IAH	8 hr 21 min	$281.00
Morning Star	2956	MIA	LAX	1-DFW	9 hr 12 min	$269.00
Tribute Air	T457	MIA	SAN	1-ORD	7 hr 41 min	$308.00
Value Air	4589	TPA	SAN	2-IAH, ORD	12 hr 11 min	$294.00
A1 Airlines	A57	MCO	LAX	1-IAH	7 hr 39 min	$303.00
Tribute Air	T390	TPA	SAN	1-DFW	7 hr 48 min	$298.00

AIRPORT CODE	CITY	STATE
TPA	Tampa	FL
IAH	Houston	TX
MEM	Memphis	TN
MCO	Orlando	FL
LAX	Los Angeles	CA
MIA	Miami	FL
DFW	Dallas	TX
SAN	San Francisco	CA
ORD	Chicago	IL
SAN	San Diego	CA

0331. Based on the charts in Fig. 15, which of the following is the correct order, from least to most expensive, for flight numbers using the cost of the flights?

    A. T349, A57, T457, 2965
    B. T598, 3475, A57, T457
    C. 4589, 3475, T390, 2965
    D. T390, T598, 3475, A57

0332. Based on the charts in Fig. 15, which of the following airport codes are in alphabetical order?

    A. IAH, LAX, ORD, MIA, MEM, SAN
    B. LAX, ORD, MEM, SFO, SAN, TPA
    C. DFW, IAH, MEM, MCO, TPA, SAN
    D. IAH, LAX, MCO, MIA, SAN, SFO

0333. Based on the charts in Fig. 15, which flight is the cheapest?

    A. T390   **C.** 2956
    B. A57   **D.** T349

0334. Based on the charts in Fig. 15, how many minutes is the shortest flight?

    A. 459 minutes   **C.** 389 minutes
    B. 549 minutes   **D.** 489 minutes

0335. Review the charts in Fig. 15. If two people spent $588.00, which flight did they take?

    A. 2965   **C.** 21A5
    B. T390   **D.** 4589

0336. Based on the charts in Fig. 15, what is the average cost per flight?

    A. $301.00   **C.** $289.00
    B. $291.90   **D.** $279.00

0337. Based on the charts in Fig. 15, what is the airport code for Miami, FL?

    A. MIM   **C.** MCO
    B. MEM   **D.** MIA

0338. Based on the charts in Fig. 15, which flight is the most expensive?

    A. 4589   **C.** T457
    B. T390   **D.** 2965

0339. Based on the charts in Fig. 15, which two cities have the same airport codes?

    A. Tampa and Dallas
    B. Houston and Dallas
    C. San Francisco and San Diego
    D. Orlando and Miami

FIGURE 16

EMPLOYEE WAGES

NAME	HOURS	RATE	WAGES
Amanda	45.00		$332.50
Carter	22.00	$7.25	$159.50
Evelyn		$6.75	$141.75
Greg	27.00	$8.15	$220.05
Inez	17.00	$8.00	$136.00
Kevin	32.25		$249.94
Maria		$7.15	$205.56
Oliver	37.00	$7.00	
Queenie	21.00	$7.50	$157.50
Seth	38.00	$8.00	$304.00
Ursula		$7.25	$322.63
Walter	32.00	$6.85	$304.83
Yvette	19.00	$7.25	$322.63

NOTE: Employees are paid time-and-a-half for working more than forty hours.

0340. Based on Fig. 16, how much is Amanda paid hourly for regular time?

    A. $7.00   **C.** $7.50
    B. $10.50   **D.** $7.25

0341. Review Fig. 16. Inez is no longer able to work. Rather than hire someone new, you decide to spread the hours among Greg, Queenie, Yvette, and Walter. What is the most cost-effective way to do this with the following limitations? Walter will work as many hours as possible, as will Greg; however, Yvette is only able to work 20 hours and Queenie can only work 25 hours.

    A. Assign Greg 4 hours, Queenie 4 hours, Yvette 1 hour, and Walter 8 hours
    B. Assign Greg 8 hours, Queenie 1 hour, Yvette 1 hour, and Walter 7 hours
    C. Assign Queenie 4 hours, Yvette 1 hour, and Walter 12 hours
    D. Assign Greg 4 hours, Yvette 1 hour, Queenie 5 hours, and Walter 7 hours

0342. Based on Fig. 16, how many hours did Evelyn work?

    A. 20.00   **C.** 22.00
    B. 21.00   **D.** 19.00

0343. Based on Fig. 16, how much does Kevin make per hour?

    A. $7.50   **C.** $7.25
    B. $7.75   **D.** $7.85

0344. Based on Fig. 16, how many hours did Maria work?

    A. 27.75   **C.** 28.25
    B. 28.75   **D.** 28.50

0345. Based on Fig. 16, how much did Oliver earn?

    A. $259.00   **C.** $245.00
    B. $217.00   **D.** $277.50

0346. Based on Fig. 16, how many hours did Ursula work?

    A. 44.50   **C.** 45.00
    B. 40.00   **D.** 41.00

0347. Review Fig. 16. You have additional work to be completed. Your top choices are Oliver and Seth. Oliver will take 8 hours to complete the task, and Seth can complete the job in half that time. Conserving money, who should you assign the task?

    A. Seth
    B. Oliver

0348. Review Fig. 16. How much more money in wages does the person who has the highest wage make than the person who has the lowest wage?

    A. $186.63   **C.** $180.88
    B. $190.75   **D.** $196.50

0349. Review Fig. 16. Excluding Amanda, who earns the lowest hourly wage?

    A. Oliver   **C.** Walter
    B. Kevin   **D.** Evelyn

FIGURE 17

TEST SCORES

Name	Verbal Reasoning	Quantitative Reasoning	Total Verbal and Quantitative Score	Analytical Writing
Marcus G	650	625	1275	4
Kimberly M	550	675	1225	4
Tom C	575	550	1125	5
Karen L	725	500	1225	6
Lisa M	700	525	1225	6
John B	650	750	1400	5
Roger V	625	750	1375	5
Theresa K	650	650	1300	5
Beverly R	675	575	1250	5
Leah T	625	550	1175	4

0350. Based on Fig. 17, did the men score higher on Verbal or Quantitative Reasoning?

    A. Verbal
    B. Quantitative

0351. Based on Fig. 17, which candidate had the strongest language performance?

    A. Beverly R   **C.** Karen L
    B. Lisa M   **D.** John B

0352. Based on Fig. 17, which candidate had the weakest combined Verbal and Quantitative Reasoning scores?

    A. Lisa M   **C.** Tom C
    B. Leah   **D.** Kimberly M

0353. Based on Fig. 17, what is the total of all of the women's Verbal Reasoning scores?

    A. 3,295   **C.** 4,025
    B. 3,275   **D.** 3,925

0354. Review Fig. 17. If you were going to select the strongest candidate for a writing program, who would you choose?

- **A.** Lisa M
- **B.** Beverly R
- **C.** John B
- **D.** Karen L

0355. What do the objects below have in common?

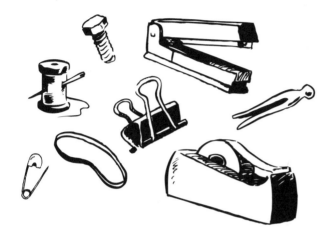

- **A.** Metal
- **B.** Sharp
- **C.** Household objects
- **D.** Fasteners

0356. Your family of five is taking a cruise. The cost is $525 per person plus a $25 gratuity per person. Taxes are 10.5 percent. You plan to save for a year. How much do you need to tuck away each week?

- **A.** $58.20
- **B.** $55.78
- **C.** $58.44
- **D.** $60.78

0357. There are 163 first-graders and 171 kindergarteners. Three children are allowed per seat, and there are thirty seats on each bus. How many buses are needed?

- **A.** Two
- **B.** Four
- **C.** Three
- **D.** One

A LITTLE BIT AT A TIME

Organization may be a natural ability or it may be a huge hurdle. Either way, it is usually easier to organize as you go rather than allowing receipts, e-mails, correspondence, etc. to pile up. Take a few minutes to label folders, sort through papers, and put things away each day rather than waiting and doing it all at once.

FIGURE 18

CHECKING ACCOUNT

CHECK #	DATE	TO	TRANSACTION	WITHDRAWAL	DEPOSIT	BALANCE
	1-May		Beginning Balance			$4,578
161	3-May	SPL	Electric	$200		$4,378
162	3-May	SP Mobile	Phone	$133		$4,245
163	3-May	Carriages	Rent	$1,500		$2,745
Debit	3-May	Shop Mart	Groceries	$182		$2,563
164	3-May	City of Sandbar	Water Co.	$150		$2,413
Debit	9-May	Tickets R Us	Concert	$94		$2,319
Debit	9-May	Blue Rays	Dinner	$41		$2,278
Credit	15-May	Paycheck	Deposit		$2,500	$4,778
ATM	15-May	Cash	Cash	$100		$4,678
	15-May		Savings	$250		$4,428
Debit	15-May	Shop Mart	Groceries	$170		$4,258
165	19-May	Teletron	Cable	$130		$4,128
166	19-May	Standard Ins	Car Ins.	$126		$4,002
167	19-May	Sandbar Bank	Credit Card	$88		$3,914
168	19-May	Sandbar Bank	Car Payment	$299		$3,615
169	19-May	US Mobile	Gas Card	$65		$3,550
Debit	23-May	Surf and Turf	Dinner	$72		$3,478
170	27-May	Shop Mart	Groceries	$182		$3,296
Debit	28-May	Good Looks	Haircut	$22		$3,274
Debit	29-May	Sandbar Bank	Bank Fee	$13		$3,261
Credit	30-May	Paycheck	Deposit		$2,500	$5,761
171	2-Jun	SPL	Electric	$212		$5,549
172	3-Jun	City of Sandbar	Water Co.	$161		$5,388
173	3-Jun	SP Mobile	Phone	$133		$5,255
174	3-Jun	Carriages	Rent	$1,500		$3,755
Debit	7-Jun	Shop Mart	Groceries	$179		$3,576
175	9-Jun	Dr. Matt	Dentist	$209		$3,367
Credit	15-Jun	Paycheck	Deposit		$2,500	$5,867
ATM	15-Jun	Cash	Cash	$100		$5,767
	15-Jun	Savings	Savings	$250		$5,517
Debit	16-Jun	JB's Steak House	Dinner	$82		$5,435
176	17-Jun	Teletron	Cable	$136		$5,299
177	17-Jun	Standard Ins	Car Ins	$126		$5,173
178	17-Jun	Sandbar Bank	Credit Card	$88		$5,085
179	17-Jun	Sandbar Bank	Car Payment	$299		$4,786
180	17-Jun	US Mobile	Gas Card	$65		$4,721
Debit	18-Jun	Shop Mart	Groceries	$198		$4,523
Debit	21-Jun	Sal's Department Store	Clothes	$232		$4,291
Debit	29-Jun	Sandbar Bank	Bank Fee	$13		$4,278
Credit	30-Jun	Paycheck	Deposit		$2,500	$6,778
Debit	30-Jun	Rivera's Café	Lunch	$26		$6,752
Debit	30-Jun	Shop Mart	Groceries	$157		$6,595

0358. Based on Fig. 18, how many checks were used in the month of June?

    A. Twenty   **C.** Twelve
    B. Seventeen   **D.** Ten

0359. Based on Fig. 18, how much money was deposited in both May and June?

    A. $1,000   **C.** $5,000
    B. $10,000   **D.** $2,500

0360. Based on Fig. 18, how much would rent be for six months?

    A. $900   **C.** $1,500
    B. $3,000   **D.** $9,000

0361. Based on Fig. 18, which check number will be used next?

    A. 160   **C.** 181
    B. 180   **D.** 186

0362. Based on Fig. 18, how much money was spent on food in the month of May?

    A. $534   **C.** $674
    B. $575   **D.** $647

0363. Based on Fig. 18, what were the total withdrawals for May 15 and June 15?

    A. $370   **C.** $870
    B. $670   **D.** $570

0364. Based on Fig. 18, if there were a 10 percent increase in pay per pay period, what would the total monthly income be?

    A. $5,050   **C.** $5,500
    B. $2,750   **D.** $11,000

0365. Based on Fig. 18 on p. 90, how much money was paid to Sandbar Bank in both May and June?

    A. $800   **C.** $400

    B. $774   **D.** $747

0366. Review Fig. 18 on p. 90. If a double payment were made on the credit card in the month of June, what would the balance be on June 30?

    A. $6,925   **C.** $6,507

    B. $6,471   **D.** $6,741

0367. Based on Fig. 18 on p. 90, what is the average monthly grocery bill?

    A. $1,070   **C.** $534

    B. $535   **D.** $182

0368. Review Fig. 18 on p. 90. If no money were spent on dinner out for the month of June, what would the ending balance be?

    A. $6,677   **C.** $6,383

    B. $6,491   **D.** $6,301

0369. Based on Fig. 18 on p. 90, which of the following dates are in order from the greatest to the least, based on withdrawals?

    A. June 3, June 17, May 19, May 15

    B. June 3, May 19, May 15, June 17

    C. May 15, May 19, June 17, June 3

    D. June 3, June 17, May 15, May 19

0370. Based on Fig. 18 on p. 90, what is the difference between withdrawals from May and June?

    A. $427   **C.** $357

    B. $429   **D.** $349

0371. Read Fig. 19. How many hours will you be driving?

    A. 77 ¾ hrs.   **C.** 52.4 hrs.

    B. 48 hrs.   **D.** 50 hrs.

FIGURE 19

You are traveling 3,250 miles and depart at 6 a.m. Your average speed is 62 mph. You plan to stop every 250 miles and rest for 15 minutes. Every third stop will be overnight for 6 hours. Hotel room costs are $150 per night plus 9.5 percent tax. You average 25 miles per gallon of gas. The cost of gas is $2.23 per gallon.

0372. Read Fig. 19. You will stop to rest after traveling for approximately what period of time?

    A. Every 4¼ hrs.   **C.** Every 3 hrs.
    B. Every 3½ hrs.   **D.** Every 4 hrs.

0373. Read Fig. 19. How much gas will you add to your tank at each stop?

    A. 11 gallons   **C.** 7 gallons
    B. 15 gallons   **D.** 10 gallons

0374. Read Fig. 19. How many stops will you make during the course of the trip?

    A. Ten   **C.** Twelve
    B. Thirteen   **D.** Four

0375. Read Fig. 19. How much will your hotel costs be?

    A. $1095.00   **C.** $492.75
    B. $657.00   **D.** $600.00

0376. Read Fig. 19. At approximately what time will you arrive at your destination?

    A. 11:45 a.m.   **C.** 7:30 a.m.
    B. 11:45 p.m.   **D.** 5:45 p.m.

0377. Read Fig. 19. How much money will you spend on gas?

    A. $223.00   **C.** $116.90
    B. $289.90   **D.** $116.85

FIGURE 20

FLOWERS

NAME	COLOR	BLOOM	ZONE	TYPE	SUN
African Lily	White, purple	July, Aug., Sept.	Vary	Bulb	Full sun, part shade
Beard-tongue	Pink, red, purple, white	June, July, Aug., Sept., Oct.	Vary	Perennial	PM shade
Begonia	Pink, red, white	June, July, Aug., Sept.	Vary	Annual	Filtered light
Chrysan-themum	Yellow, orange	Aug., Sept.	Vary	Perennial	Full sun
Crocus	Lilac	Dec., Jan., Feb., Mar., Apr.	US, MS	Bulb	Full sun, part shade
Daffodil	White, yellow	Jan., Feb., Mar., Apr., May	US, MS, LS, CS	Bulb	Full sun, part shade
English Violet	Purple, pink, white	Mar., Apr., May	Vary	Perennial	Vary
Geranium	Red, white, pink	May, June, July, Aug., Sept.	US, MS, LS	Perennial	Full sun
Gladiolus	Red	May, June, July, Aug., Sept.	MS, LS, CS	Bulb	Full sun
Glory of the Snow	Pink, blue	Feb., Mar., Apr.	US, MS	Bulb	Full sun
Goldenrod	Yellow	July, Aug.	US, MS, LS, CS	Perennial	Full sun
Hosta	White, purple	June, July, Sept.	US, MS, LS	Perennial	Full sun
Impatiens	Pink, purple, red, white	June, July, Aug., Sept., Oct.	US, MS, LS, CS, TS	Annual	Vary
Ornamen-tal Onion	Purple-pink	Apr., May, June, July	Vary	Bulb	Full sun, part shade
Pansy	Purple	Apr., May, June, July, Aug., Sept.	Vary	Annual	Vary
Petunia	Pink, red, white, purple	June, July, Aug., Sept.	US, MS, LS, CS, TS	Annual	Full sun
Sunflower	Yellow	June, July, Aug., Sept.	Vary	Annual	Full sun
Zinnia	Red, yellow, pink, orange, white	July, Aug., Sept., Oct.	US, MS, LS, CS, TS	Annual	Full sun

0378. Review Fig. 20. You live in the MS and are planting a bulb garden. Your main objective is to extend the blooming period as long as possible. Which month(s) will you not have blooms in your garden?

    A. Nov.   **C.** Oct.
    B. May and Oct.   **D.** Oct. and Nov.

0379. Review Fig. 20. You decide to plant only white flowers in your annual garden. Which flowers will you plant?

    A. Impatiens, Begonia, and Petunia
    B. Zinnia, Impatiens, Begonia, and Petunia
    C. Geranium, Hosta, English Violet, and Beardtongue
    D. Zinnia, Impatiens, Petunia, Begonia, and Beardtongue

0380. Review Fig. 20. Your garden will be a mix of bulbs, perennials, and annuals. However, you intend to plant only white, pink, and purple flowers that strictly require full sun and that bloom in February, March, and April. Which flowers will you include in your garden?

    A. Pink Glory of the Snow
    B. African Lily, Daffodil, English Violet
    C. Glory of the Snow, Pansy
    D. Pansy, Glory of the Snow, English Violet

0381. Based on Fig. 20, which months will your perennial garden bloom if you plant all of the selections?

    A. All months except Nov., Dec., and Jan.
    B. All months except Dec. and Jan.
    C. All months except Jan., Feb., Nov., and Dec.
    D. All months except Oct. and Nov.

ORGANIZATION OPTIONS

There's an old adage, "There's more than one way to skin a cat." The same is true for organization. Usually there are multiple ways to organize material, and the trick is to choose the most efficient and most logical way for you. For example, your garage might currently be organized so that each specific type of tool is located in its own place—all of the hammers placed together, all of the Phillips head screwdrivers together, etc. However, you might find it more efficient to have a toolbox that only has your favorite screwdriver, one hammer, one wrench, and a few other commonly used tools in it, so you don't have to run back to the garage each time you need a slightly different tool.

0382. Based on Fig. 20 on pgs. 94–95, which plants will not grow in the Coastal South?

   A. Glory of the Snow, Crocus, Geranium, and Hosta
   B. Geranium and Hosta
   C. Crocus and Hosta
   D. Geranium, Hosta, and Crocus

0383. Review Fig. 20 on pgs. 94–95. Your garden will consist of yellow perennials and annuals. Which flowers will be included?

   A. Chrysanthemum and Goldenrod
   B. Sunflower, Chrysanthemum, Daffodil, and Goldenrod
   C. Goldenrod, Chrysanthemum, and Daffodil
   D. Zinnia, Sunflower, Chrysanthemum, and Goldenrod

0384. Review Fig. 20 on pgs. 94–95. You are planning a mixed-bed garden. You will alternate rows of flowers with annuals, perennials, and bulbs, without repeating a flower. You will alternate colors with white, pink, red, purple, and the front rows will be the flowers that bloom earliest in the year and for the longest months possible, requiring full sun or variable. (Hint: Create eight rows.) What will be the order of the flowers if you create this garden?

   A. Impatiens, English Violet, Gladiolus, Pansy, Geranium, Glory of the Snow, Petunia, and Hosta
   B. Petunia, English Violet, Gladiolus, Pansy, Geranium, Glory of the Snow, Petunia, and Beardtongue
   C. Impatiens, English Violet, Gladiolus, Zinnia, Geranium, Glory of the Snow, Petunia, and Beardtongue
   D. Impatiens, English Violet, Gladiolus, Petunia, Geranium, African Lily, Begonia, and Beardtongue

0385. Based on Fig. 20 on pgs. 94–95, which of the bulbs bloom white in August?

   A. Gladiolus   **C.** African Lily
   B. Daffodil   **D.** Beardtongue

0386. Based on Fig. 20 on pgs. 94–95, which grouping of flowers has the most varied colors?

   A. Annuals and Perennials
   B. Annuals
   C. Perennials
   D. Bulbs

FIGURE 21

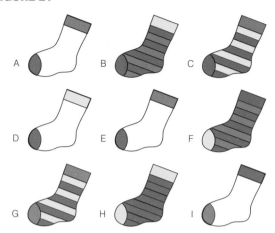

0387. Based on Fig. 20 on pgs. 94–95, which is the only flower colored purple-pink?

    A. Petunia   **C.** Ornamental Onion
    B. Impatiens   **D.** English Violet

0388. Based on Fig. 21, which two socks match exactly?

    A. A and C   **C.** F and B
    B. C and D   **D.** A and E

0389. Based on Fig. 21, which socks have toe and band colors that are reversed?

    A. B and C   **C.** A and F
    B. D and C   **D.** B and F

0390. Based on Fig. 21, how many socks have the same color in the toe area?

    A. Two   **C.** Four
    B. Three   **D.** One

0391. Based on Fig. 21, which socks have all four colors in them?

    A. C, H, F   **C.** G, C, H
    B. B, H, G   **D.** B, F, C

FIGURE 22

GLOBAL TIMES

Greenwich Time	5:00 p.m.
Hong Kong, China	+ 8:00
Sydney, Australia	=
Toronto, Canada	- 5:00
London, England	=
New York, New York	- 5:00
Tokyo, Japan	+ 9:00
Rio de Janeiro, Brazil	- 3:00
Anchorage, Alaska	- 9:00
Honolulu, Hawaii	- 10:00
Los Angeles, California	- 8:00
Mexico City, Mexico	- 6:00
Melbourne, Australia	+11:00
Rome, Italy	+ 1:00
Cairo, Egypt	+ 2:00
Paris, France	+ 1:00

0392. Review Fig. 22. If Greenwich Time is 11:00 p.m. on Tuesday, what day and time would it be in Melbourne?

    A. 9:00 p.m. on Tuesday
    B. 10:00 a.m. on Wednesday
    C. 10:00 p.m. on Tuesday
    D. 8:00 a.m. on Wednesday

0393. Review Fig. 22. Which of the following cities are in alphabetical order according to the country they are in?

    A. London, Hong Kong, Paris, Sydney
    B. Anchorage, Rome, Paris, Tokyo
    C. Toronto, Paris, Tokyo, Honolulu
    D. Melbourne, Mexico City, Sydney, Toronto

0394. Review Fig. 22. If it is 3:00 a.m. Greenwich Time, in which of the following cities will it also be 3:00 a.m.?

    A. Tokyo, Japan
    B. London, England and Sydney, Australia
    C. Paris, France
    D. Toronto, Canada

0395. Review Fig. 22. If it is 5:00 p.m. in New York, what time is it in Los Angeles?

  A. 8:00 a.m.   **C.** 2:00 a.m.
  B. 8:00 p.m.   **D.** 2:00 p.m.

0396. Based on Fig. 22, which place is only two hours different from Greenwich Time?

  A. Cairo, Egypt   **C.** Sydney, Australia
  B. Rome, Italy   **D.** Paris, France

0397. Review Fig. 22. If it is 3:00 p.m. in Egypt, what time would Greenwich Time be?

  A. 1:00 a.m.   **C.** 1:00 p.m.
  B. 3:00 a.m.   **D.** 2:00 p.m.

0398. Review Fig. 22. If you wake up in Tokyo at 8:00 a.m. and want to call your spouse in Toronto, what time will it be in Canada?

  A. 8:00 p.m.   **C.** 10:00 a.m.
  B. 6:00 p.m.   **D.** 6:00 a.m.

0399. You're having a party and plan for 23 people. You will need 8 oz of beverage for each person. How many gallons of beverages will you need?

  A. 4   **C.** 5
  B. 2   **D.** 3

0400. Review Fig. 22. If your nine-hour flight leaves New York at 5 p.m., what time will you land in Rome (local time)?

  A. 3:00 p.m.   **C.** 2:00 p.m.
  B. 8:00 a.m.   **D.** 7:00 a.m.

ORGANIZATION

0392–
0400

MEMORY

IMMEDIATE AND DELAYED RECALL & REMOTE MEMORY

Memory is seated in the temporal lobes but is processed throughout the brain. It is a complex process that includes the absorption of new information, meaningful storage of the information, and the ability to retrieve that information at a later time. There are multiple memory systems throughout the brain.

There are separate memory systems for Vision, Language, Motor memory, as well as memory for Smell, Taste, and Touch. With multiple memory systems located throughout the brain, there is the possibility of making multiple copies of a memory within the different regions of the brain. For example, memory for musical tone is stored on the opposite side of the brain memory from sentence structure. So, if you sing your grocery list out loud, you will have encoded the list in Verbal memory, Music memory, and Motor memory. This will make it a little more difficult to forget what you need at the grocery store!

The concept of memory is often broken down into time. Immediate memory is the ability to recall something immediately after it is heard or seen. Long-term memory or "delayed recall" is the ability to recall that same information after a set period of time—usually measured in minutes or hours. Remote memory is memory from long ago, such as childhood memories or memories from early adulthood.

Another type of memory is Incidental memory, which is the memory for information that you have been exposed to without a prior request to actively remember the information. In other words, Incidental memory is what happens to be "encoded" or memorized by chance. Working memory (also addressed under Executive Functions) is the data within your awareness that you are currently focused on and purposefully trying to remember.

All of these memory systems have two primary functions. The first is the "encoding," or the making, of the memory, and the second is the "retrieval," or the reclamation, of the memory. It is in the retrieval that most people begin to notice slippage. (By the way, "metamemory" is a person's memory of their own memory—basically, remembering that you forget!)

Within this chapter, you will be challenged to improve your memory with tasks that draw on Immediate and Delayed Recall as well as Remote memory. There are also tasks that coach you through memory techniques, such as using elaboration, acronyms, and association. As you exercise your brain and further apply these techniques in real life, you will begin to see improvements in your ability to retain and recall information.

FIGURE 1

Mary Sue Ellen is a teacher at Westbrook Elementary. She has been working at the same school for 22 years. On her way to work, Mary usually takes Interstate 95, gets off at exit 56/Tamiami Trail, makes a right, and follows HWY 27 all the way to her office. It takes 36 minutes to get there. This morning, however, Mary decided to try a new route. She thought if she took Interstate 4 to exit 54/Colonial Drive, made a left, and followed HWY 27 all the way to work, it might be quicker. When Mary got to Colonial Drive, she noticed that the car in front of her was swerving back and forth, so she decided to slow down a little. A few minutes later, the car crashed into the median and caused Mary to run right into the back of the car. When the man driving got out of the car, he was clearly suffering from dementia. Mary called the police to investigate the accident. Shortly thereafter, the ambulance arrived, and the gentleman was transported to the hospital. Fortunately, there were no physical injuries.

0401. Read Fig. 1, then answer the question without referring back to the story. [STOP] What road does Mary work on?

  A. Interstate 95   **C.** HWY 27
  B. Interstate 4   **D.** HWY 26

0402. Read Fig. 1, then answer the question without referring back to the story. [STOP] What was the name of the school where Mary worked?

  A. Westbrook Elementary
  B. Westbrook High School
  C. Westwood Elementary
  D. Wonderwood Elementary

0403. Read Fig. 1, then answer the question without referring back to the story. [STOP] What did the man crash into?

  A. The median   **C.** A dog
  B. A person   **D.** Another car

0404. Read Fig. 1, then answer the question without referring back to the story. [STOP] What did Mary do after the accident?

  A. She yelled at the man
  B. She drove on to work
  C. She didn't do anything
  D. She called the police

0405. Read Fig. 1, then answer the question without referring back to the story. [STOP] What did Mary do when she noticed the car was swerving?

    A. She turned at the next road
    B. She sped up
    C. She slowed down
    D. She yelled at the man in front of her

0406. Read Fig. 1, then answer the question without referring back to the story. [STOP] How long has Mary been working at Westbrook Elementary?

    A. 22 years
    B. 10 years
    C. 23 years
    D. She doesn't work at Westbrook Elementary

0407. Read Fig. 1, then answer the question without referring back to the story. [STOP] Why did Mary decide to take a new route to work?

    A. She thought it might be quicker
    B. She had to
    C. There was a traffic jam
    D. Because her friend told her to

0408. Read Fig. 1, then answer the question without referring back to the story. [STOP] Why did the ambulance come?

    A. The man was physically injured
    B. Mary called the police, and the man was suffering from dementia
    C. Mary was physically injured
    D. A bystander was injured

0409. Read Fig. 1, then answer the question without referring back to the story. [STOP] What route does Mary usually take to work?

    A. Interstate 95, gets off at exit 55, and makes a right.
    B. Interstate 95, gets off at exit 56/Tamiami Trail, makes a right, and follows HWY 27
    C. Interstate 4 to exit 54/ Colonial Dr, makes a left, and follows HWY 27
    D. Interstate 95, gets off at exit 56/Tamiami Trail, makes a left, and follows HWY 27

MEMORY

0401–
0409

FIGURE 2

Bobby Butler works as a bread baker in Banquet, Iowa. On Monday morning, he made 7 batches of sourdough using 4 bags of flour. He new he had to order new flour for next Tuesday when he would be making 21 batches of sourdough for the Bail Bondsmen's Brunch. On the Monday prior to that Tuesday, Bobby's coworker Billy Barber, who Bobby first met at Bartender College, made 12 batches of buttery biscuits for the upcoming breakfast to honor the Brattice Builder's Bureau. Billy used twelve bags of Bobby's flour.

0410. Read Fig. 1 on p. 102, then answer the question without referring back to the story. [STOP] How long does it take Mary to get to work on her usual route?

    A. 35 minutes   **C.** 60 minutes
    B. 36 minutes   **D.** 45 minutes

0411. Read Fig. 2, then answer the question without referring back to the story. [STOP] How many bags of flour will Bobby be short because Billy used 12 bags?

    A. 8   **C.** 9
    B. 21   **D.** 12

0412. Read Fig. 2, then answer the question without referring back to the story. [STOP] What was Billy's last name?

    A. Baker   **C.** Butler
    B. Barber   **D.** Builder

0413. Read Fig. 2, then answer the question without referring back to the story. [STOP] What was Mr. Butler baking?

    A. Buns   **C.** Brattice
    B. Biscuits   **D.** Sourdough

0414. Read Fig. 2, then answer the question without referring back to the story. [STOP] The banquet was for what group?

    A. Barber's Bureau
    B. Brattice Builder's
    C. There was no banquet
    D. Bail Bondsmen's

0415. Read Fig. 2, then answer the question without referring back to the story. [STOP] What was Mr. Barber's first name?

    A. Bailey   **C.** Bobby
    B. Billy   **D.** Brandon

0416. Read Fig. 2, then answer the question without referring back to the story. [STOP] For what event was Bobby baking?

    A. Butler's brunch
    B. Bail Bondsmen's Brunch
    C. Brattice Builder's Bureau
    D. Barber's Bureau Breakfast

0417. Read Fig. 2, then answer the question without referring back to the story. [STOP] For what event was Billy baking?

    A. Butler's Brunch
    B. Brattice Builder's Bureau
    C. Bail Bondsmen's Brunch
    D. Barber's Bureau Breakfast

0418. Read Fig. 2, then answer the question without referring back to the story. [STOP] Who will be baking on Tuesday?

    A. Bobby and Billy
    B. Billy
    C. Bobby
    D. Barber

0419. Read Fig. 2, then answer the question without referring back to the story. [STOP] Which word was used incorrectly?

    A. Brattice   **C.** New
    B. Flower   **D.** Know

0420. Read Fig. 2, then answer the question without referring back to the story. [STOP] How many bags of flour per batch of buttery biscuits did Billy use?

    A. 12   **C.** 2
    B. 1   **D.** None

MEMORY

0410–0420

FIGURE 3

Joshua E. Brown (Jeb) is a political science major at the University of Tulsa in Tulsa, Oklahoma. The university is a private school that was founded by the Presbyterian Church in 1894 and is currently ranked no. 83 among national universities. In addition to his studies, Jeb is an avid reader of science fiction and enjoys playing soccer, tennis, squash, and croquet. Jeb's buddies from his hometown of Mobile, Alabama, attend college at Tulane University in New Orleans. Jeb's friends are Evan, Edward, and Eve. Evan plays football for the Green Wave and is a biological science major; Edward plays baseball and is enrolled in the school of science and engineering. Eve is a liberal arts major and participates in women's golf, tennis, and volleyball. Evan, Eve, Edward, and Jeb all attended the Methodist church in Mobile and sang in the church choir. Secretly, Jeb is enrolled in a dance squad, where he utilizes his fancy footwork from his sports background.

0421. Read Fig. 3, then answer the question without referring back to the story. [STOP] What religion was Jeb affiliated with?

    A. Methodist   **C.** Presbyterian
    B. Lutheran   **D.** Catholic

0422. Read Fig. 3, then answer the question without referring back to the story. [STOP] What sport did two of the four friends have in common?

    A. Tennis   **C.** Basketball
    B. Baseball   **D.** Golf

0423. Read Fig. 3, then answer the question without referring back to the story. [STOP] What was Eve's major?

    A. Political Science
    B. Biology
    C. Liberal Arts
    D. Engineering

0424. Read Fig. 3, then answer the question without referring back to the story. [STOP] What was Jeb's hometown?

    A. New Orleans   **C.** Tulsa
    B. Mobile   **D.** Little Rock

0425. Read Fig. 3, then answer the question without referring back to the story. [STOP] What rank was the University of Tulsa in the listing of national colleges?

A. 83 **C.** 95
B. 105 **D.** 38

0426. Read Fig. 3, then answer the question without referring back to the story. [STOP] What was Jeb's middle name?

A. Eve **C.** Edward
B. Evan **D.** None of these

0427. Read Fig. 3, then answer the question without referring back to the story. [STOP] Jeb was an avid reader of what subject?

A. Biology **C.** Science fiction
B. Nonfiction **D.** Religion

0428. Read Fig. 3, then answer the question without referring back to the story. [STOP] What was the name of the football team Evan played for?

A. Green Wave **C.** Big Wave
B. Green Tide **D.** Golden Hurricane

0429. Read Fig. 3, then answer the question without referring back to the story. [STOP] In which year was the University of Tulsa founded?

A. 1984 **C.** 1804
B. 1894 **D.** 1884

0430. Read Fig. 3, then answer the question without referring back to the story. [STOP] What did the four friends all do together?

A. Play football
B. Dance squad
C. Sing in church choir
D. Attend college at University of Tulsa

MEMORY

0421–
0430

FIGURE 4

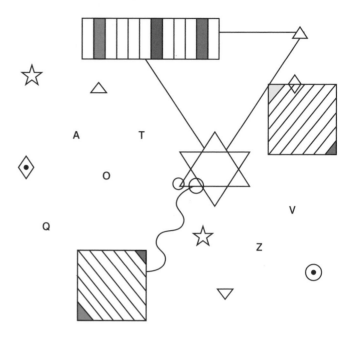

0431. Which planet is third from the sun?

    A. Venus   **C.** Earth
    B. Mars   **D.** Mercury

0432. You need to buy stuffing, oatmeal, raisins, apples, and bread for toast at the store. Which of the following is the simplest acronym to help you remember your list?

    A. Star-O   **C.** ROAST
    B. OARS-T   **D.** O-RATS

0433. You need the following items from the hardware store: anvil, tape, hose, mallet, screwdriver, and tacks. Which of the following mnemonics will help you remember all of these items?

    A. Tolls Are My Secret Talent
    B. Hardware Things Are Silly Things
    C. Stuff That Helps Administer Messes
    D. Money To Spend At The Hardware

FIGURE 5

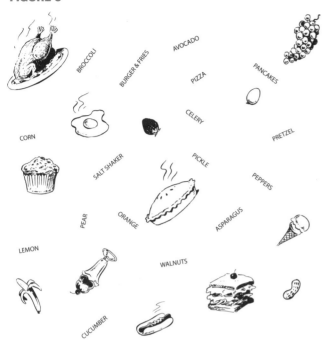

0434. On February 4, you have a meeting from 6 to 8. Which of the following is a cheerful way to remember your appointment?

    A. I have a date from 6 to 8
    B. Count by 2s up to 8
    C. Month 2, Day 4, Scheduled 6 to 8
    D. 2-4-6-8! Who do we appreciate?

0435. You need coffee, bread, cookies, sugar, butter, and milk. Which of the following is the best pairing of these words to help you remember your list?

    A. Butter and Milk, Bread and Sugar, Coffee and Butter
    B. Bread and Butter, Coffee and Milk, Sugar and Cookies
    C. Bread and Butter, Coffee and Sugar, Milk and Cookies
    D. Cookies and Milk, Bread and Sugar, Coffee and Butter

0436. Why does citronella repel mosquitoes?

    A. It irritates their feet
    B. It is poisonous
    C. It causes their wings to fall off
    D. It kills them

R.A.R.E.

To streamline your memory, try the RARE Approach (Mason and Kohn, 2001). RARE stands for Relax, Attend, Repeat, and Envision. These simple steps improve encoding. Take just a moment, and relax your mind and body. Purposefully place your attention on whatever items you may want to remember. Repeat the items to be remembered. Finally, envision the items with all of the senses (sight, smell, taste, touch, and hearing).

0437. You have one minute to review Fig. 4 on p. 108. Press the ⏻ on the Coach, then answer the question as quickly as you can. [STOP] Which of the following squares represents the square in the bottom left of the diagram?

A.   C.

B.   D.

0438. You have one minute to review Fig. 4 on p. 108. Press the ⏻ on the Coach, then answer the question as quickly as you can. [STOP] How many stars were in the diagram?

A. Two   **C.** One
B. Three   **D.** Four

0439. You have one minute to review Fig. 4 on p. 108. Press the ⏻ on the Coach, then answer the question as quickly as you can. [STOP] What shape bisected the top line of the square in the upper right of the diagram?

A. Square   **C.** Diamond
B. Triangle   **D.** Star

0440. You have one minute to review Fig. 4 on p. 108. Press the ⏻ on the Coach, then answer the question as quickly as you can. [STOP] Within the large rectangle, what color was the middle rectangle?

A. Green   **C.** Blue
B. Red   **D.** Yellow

0441. You have one minute to review Fig. 4 on p. 108. Press the ⏻ on the Coach, then answer the question as quickly as you can. [STOP] Which of the following triangles resembles the triangle at the bottom of the picture?

A. △   C. ▷

B. ▽   D. ◁

0442. You have one minute to review Fig. 4 on p. 108. Press the ⏻ on the Coach, then answer the question as quickly as you can. [STOP] How many shapes had a dot in the center?

    A. One   **C.** Two
    B. Three   **D.** None

0443. You have one minute to review Fig. 4 on p. 108. Press the ⏻ on the Coach, then answer the question as quickly as you can. [STOP] Which of the following letters was *not* in the diagram?

    A. W   **C.** A
    B. V   **D.** Z

0444. You have one minute to review Fig. 4 on p. 108. Press the ⏻ on the Coach, then answer the question as quickly as you can. [STOP] Which of the following letters was included in the diagram?

    A. M   **C.** Z
    B. W   **D.** H

0445. You have one minute to review Fig. 4 on p. 108. Press the ⏻ on the Coach, then answer the question as quickly as you can. [STOP] How many arrows were included in the diagram?

    A. Two   **C.** Three
    B. One   **D.** None

0446. You have one minute to review Fig. 4 on p. 108. Press the ⏻ on the Coach, then answer the question as quickly as you can. [STOP] Which of the following diagrams correctly represents how the middle figure was connected to the figure on the bottom left of the diagram?

    A.   **C.**

    B.   **D.**

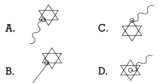

0447. You have thirty seconds to review Fig. 5 on p. 109. Press the ⏱ on the Coach, then answer the question as quickly as you can. [STOP] Which fruit was in the upper-right-hand corner of the diagram?

    A. Banana   **C.** Strawberry
    B. Cherries   **D.** Grapes

0448. You have thirty seconds to review Fig. 5 on p. 109. Press the ⏱ on the Coach, then answer the question as quickly as you can. [STOP] Which of the following vegetables was *not* included?

    A. Green beans   **C.** Asparagus
    B. Celery   **D.** Corn

0449. You have thirty seconds to review Fig. 5 on p. 109. Press the ⏱ on the Coach, then answer the question as quickly as you can. [STOP] What kind of nut was included?

    A. Peanut and walnut
    B. Hickory nut
    C. Peanut
    D. Pecan

0450. You have thirty seconds to review Fig. 5 on p. 109. Press the ⏱ on the Coach, then answer the question as quickly as you can. [STOP] How many eggs were shown?

    A. Three   **C.** None
    B. One   **D.** Two

0451. You have thirty seconds to review Fig. 5 on p. 109. Press the ⏱ on the Coach, then answer the question as quickly as you can. [STOP] What was shown in the middle of the diagram?

    A. Pie   **C.** Lemon
    B. Asparagus   **D.** Turkey

0452. You have thirty seconds to review Fig. 5 on p. 109. Press the ⏱ on the Coach, then answer the question as quickly as you can. [STOP] How many desserts were displayed?

    A. Two   **C.** Three
    B. Four   **D.** One

0453. You have thirty seconds to review Fig. 5 on p. 109. Press the ⟳ on the Coach, then answer the question as quickly as you can. [STOP] What seasoning was included?

    A. Pepper   **C.** Salt
    B. Sugar   **D.** Garlic

0454. You have thirty seconds to review Fig. 5 on p. 109. Press the ⟳ on the Coach, then answer the question as quickly as you can. [STOP] Which of the following fruits were *not* included?

    A. Orange   **C.** Apple
    B. Pear   **D.** Lemon

0455. You have thirty seconds to review Fig. 5 on p. 109. Press the ⟳ on the Coach, then answer the question as quickly as you can. [STOP] How many sandwiches were included?

    A. Four   **C.** One
    B. Two   **D.** Three

0456. You have thirty seconds to review Fig. 5 on p. 109. Press the ⟳ on the Coach, then answer the question as quickly as you can. [STOP] What was in the bottom left corner of the diagram?

    A. Banana
    B. Ice cream sundae
    C. Peanut
    D. Muffin

0457. Review Fig. 5 on p. 109, then count to 50 before answering the question. [STOP] Which of the following breakfast foods was *not* shown?

    A. Muffin
    B. Scrambled eggs
    C. Fried egg
    D. Pancakes

0458. Review Fig. 5 on p. 109, then say the alphabet before answering the question. [STOP] Which of the following vegetables was included?

    A. Green beans   **C.** Peas
    B. Avocado   **D.** Cauliflower

0459. Review Fig. 5 on p. 109, then name ten different animals before answering the question. [stop] Which of the following desserts was depicted?

    A. Cobbler   **C.** Banana split
    B. Cake   **D.** Pie

0460. Review Fig. 5 on p. 109, then count backward from 20 to 1 before answering the question. [stop] What was in the bottom right corner of the diagram?

    A. Sandwich   **C.** Ice cream cone
    B. Banana   **D.** Peanut

0461. Review Fig. 5 on p. 109, then spell your first name backwards before answering the question. [stop] Did the hot dog have any condiments on it?

    A. Yes
    B. No

0462. At what temperature does water freeze?

    A. -32 degrees F   **C.** 17 degrees F
    B. 0 degrees F   **D.** 32 degrees F

0463. What makes plants green?

    A. Chloroform   **C.** Cholera
    B. Chlorine   **D.** Chlorophyll

0464. What religion is associated with the advent of Valentine's Day?

    A. Catholicism   **C.** Lutheranism
    B. Protestantism   **D.** Judaism

0465. Without looking, what shape is in the upper-left-hand corner of this page?

    A. A circle   **C.** A triangle
    B. A diamond   **D.** A square

FIGURE 6

0466.   What is the longest river in the world?

    A. Mississippi River
    B. Amazon River
    C. Nile River
    D. Yangtze River

0467.   What is the longest cave in the world?

    A. Carlsbad Cavern
    B. Lechuguilla Cave
    C. Hellhole
    D. Mammoth Cave

0468.   Who wrote *The Merchant of Venice*?

    A. Steinbeck
    B. Shakespeare
    C. Hemingway
    D. Twain

METHOD OF LOCI

The Method of Loci is an ancient encoding strategy where items to be remembered are associated with pre-learned locations. Choose ten specific locations, and memorize them. You may want to picture yourself entering your house. The first place you come to is the porch—that will be the first location. The second place you enter is your foyer (location no. 2). The third place you enter is the dining room (location no. 3). Create ten such locations and always review them in the same order. Now, place each item you want to remember in a specific location. So, for example, if your first errand of the day is to go to the bank, picture an ATM machine on your porch. If the next errand is going to the post office, mentally place several large bags of mail in your foyer. Finally, let's say that you must meet your friend Sally for lunch. Picture Sally in the dining room pigging out on mashed potatoes. The more ridiculous the images the better—they'll help you remember.

0469. You have one minute to review Fig. 6 on p. 115. Press the ⏱ on the Coach, then answer the question as quickly as you can. [STOP] Which of the following illuminating objects was shown?

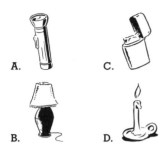

A.   C.

B.   D.

0470. You have one minute to review Fig. 6 on p. 115. Press the ⏱ on the Coach, then answer the question as quickly as you can. [STOP] On the traffic light, which light was lit?

    A. Green   **C.** Red
    B. Yellow   **D.** None

0471. You have one minute to review Fig. 6 on p. 115. Press the ⏱ on the Coach, then answer the question as quickly as you can. [STOP] Which of the following objects from the sea was shown?

    A. Dolphin   **C.** Sea turtle
    B. Starfish   **D.** Sea horse

0472. You have one minute to review Fig. 6 on p. 115. Press the ⏱ on the Coach, then answer the question as quickly as you can. [STOP] Which eating utensil was pictured?

    A. Spoon   **C.** Knife
    B. Fork   **D.** Straw

0473. You have one minute to review Fig. 6 on p. 115. Press the ⏱ on the Coach, then answer the question as quickly as you can. [STOP] How many sharp objects were included?

    A. One   **C.** Four
    B. Three   **D.** Five

0474. You have one minute to review Fig. 6 on p. 115. Press the ⏱ on the Coach, then answer the question as quickly as you can. [STOP] Did the toaster have a piece of bread in it?

    A. Yes
    B. No

0475. You have one minute to review Fig. 6 on p. 115. Press the ⏱ on the Coach, then answer the question as quickly as you can. [STOP] How many of the items circulate air?

    A. One   **C.** None
    B. Two   **D.** Three

0476. You have one minute to review Fig. 6 on p. 115. Press the ⏱ on the Coach, then answer the question as quickly as you can. [STOP] Which of the following musical instruments was pictured?

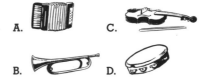

    A.   **C.**

    B.   **D.**

0477. You have one minute to review Fig. 6 on p. 115. Press the ⏱ on the Coach, then answer the question as quickly as you can. [STOP] How many weapons were pictured?

    A. Two   **C.** Three
    B. One   **D.** None

0478. You have one minute to review Fig. 6 on p. 115. Press the ⏱ on the Coach, then answer the question as quickly as you can. [STOP] Did the radio have a cord attached?

    A. Yes
    B. No

0479. You have one minute to review Fig. 6 on p. 115. Press the ↻ on the Coach, then answer the question as quickly as you can. [STOP] What color was at the top of the safety pin?

    A. Red   **C.** Green
    B. Blue   **D.** White

0480. You have one minute to review Fig. 6 on p. 115. Press the ↻ on the Coach, then answer the question as quickly as you can. [STOP] What object was in the upper-left-hand corner of the picture?

    A. Axe   **C.** Money bag
    B. Cell phone **D.** Typewriter

0481. You have one minute to review Fig. 6 on p. 115. Press the ↻ on the Coach, then answer the question as quickly as you can. [STOP] Which of the following items was *not* pictured?

    A. Tire   **C.** Doughnuts
    B. Ink well   **D.** Skull

0482. You have one minute to review Fig. 6 on p. 115. Press the ↻ on the Coach, then answer the question as quickly as you can. [STOP] What color was the yo-yo?

    A. Blue   **C.** Red
    B. Green   **D.** Yellow

0483. You have one minute to review Fig. 6 on p. 115. Press the ↻ on the Coach, then answer the question as quickly as you can. [STOP] Which of the following items was pictured?

    A. Balloon   **C.** Iron
    B. Basket   **D.** Rolling pin

0484. Without looking, how is the page number on this page different from all other pages in this book?

    A. It is underlined
    B. It is upside down
    C. It is backward
    D. It is omitted

MEMORY

0474–0484

FIGURE 7

0485. Without looking, what is the title of this book?

    A. *Brain Basic Course*
    B. *Brain Boot Camp*
    C. *Brain Basics*
    D. *Brain Busters*

0486. When was the first U.S. coast-to-coast telephone established?

    A. 1926   **C.** 1915
    B. 1930   **D.** 1945

0487. What color was Coca-Cola originally?

    A. Green   **C.** Clear
    B. Brown   **D.** Red

0488. Since the beginning of the modern-day Olympics, which countries are the only two to participate every year?

    A. Greece and Australia
    B. Greece and England
    C. America and Athens
    D. China and America

FIGURE 8

FLOAT ⟷ TREE
HORSE ⟷ ROSE
PLANT ⟷ CHAIR
SOFA ⟷ CUP
GUITAR ⟷ ROCK

0489. Carefully read the word pairs list in Fig. 8 aloud three times, then answer the question without referring back to the list. [STOP] Which word was paired with "Sofa"?

A. Cup   **C.** Fig
B. Car   **D.** Toe

0490. Carefully read the word pairs list in Fig. 8 aloud three times, then answer the question without referring back to the list. [STOP] Which word was paired with "Float"?

A. Mirror   **C.** Arm
B. Pen   **D.** Tree

0491. Carefully read the word pairs list in Fig. 8 aloud three times, then answer the question without referring back to the list. [STOP] Which of the following words rhymes with the word that was paired with "Plant"?

A. Bear   **C.** Booth
B. Tar   **D.** Hog

0492. Carefully read the word pairs list in Fig. 8 aloud three times, then answer the question without referring back to the list. [STOP] Which word was paired with "Horse"?

A. Hose   **C.** Rose
B. Fence   **D.** Moon

0493. Carefully read the word pairs list in Fig. 8 aloud three times, then answer the question without referring back to the list. [STOP] Which of the following words rhymes with the word that was paired with "Guitar"?

A. Bird   **C.** Lock
B. Big   **D.** Farm

MEMORY

0485–0493

121

0494. You have thirty seconds to review Fig. 7 on p. 120. Press the ⏱ on the Coach, then answer the question as quickly as you can. [STOP] Which animal was pictured upside down?

    A. Bat   **C.** Lobster

    B. Bird   **D.** Fox

0495. You have thirty seconds to review Fig. 7 on p. 120. Press the ⏱ on the Coach, then answer the question as quickly as you can. [STOP] How many sea animals were shown?

    A. Two   **C.** Four

    B. Three   **D.** Five

0496. You have thirty seconds to review Fig. 7 on p. 120. Press the ⏱ on the Coach, then answer the question as quickly as you can. [STOP] Which animal was in the center of the picture?

    A. Penguin   **C.** Kangaroo

    B. Giraffe   **D.** Octopus

0497. You have thirty seconds to review Fig. 7 on p. 120. Press the ⏱ on the Coach, then answer the question as quickly as you can. [STOP] How many of the animals shown were winged?

    A. Four   **C.** One

    B. Three   **D.** Two

0498. You have thirty seconds to review Fig. 7 on p. 120. Press the ⏱ on the Coach, then answer the question as quickly as you can. [STOP] The dog was shown to the right of which animal?

    A. Lobster   **C.** Fish

    B. Kangaroo **D.** Pelican

0499. You have thirty seconds to review Fig. 7 on p. 120. Press the ⏱ on the Coach, then answer the question as quickly as you can. [STOP] How many of the animals had tails?

    A. Three   **C.** Five

    B. Four   **D.** Six

FIGURE 9

PHONE ←→ HOSE BEACH ←→ FIG
FOLDER ←→ MIRROR DISH ←→ ECHO
FRAME ←→ PEN BOAT ←→ ARM
CASTLE ←→ FENCE RABBIT ←→ MOON
LOCK ←→ BIRD TRUCK ←→ FOREST

0500. Carefully read the word pairs list in Fig. 9 aloud three times, then answer the question without referring back to the list. [STOP] Which word was paired with "Lock"?

  A. Bird   **C.** Dog
  B. Car   **D.** Rock

0501. Carefully read the word pairs list in Fig. 9 aloud three times, then answer the question without referring back to the list. [STOP] Which word was paired with "Dish"?

  A. Cup   **C.** Tooth
  B. Rock   **D.** Echo

0502. Carefully read the word pairs list in Fig. 9 aloud three times, then answer the question without referring back to the list. [STOP] Which of the following words rhymes with the word that was paired with "Frame"?

  A. Ten   **C.** Lock
  B. Pet   **D.** Bar

0503. Carefully read the word pairs list in Fig. 9 aloud three times, then answer the question without referring back to the list. [STOP] Which of the following words rhymes with the word that was paired with "Rabbit"?

  A. Pup   **C.** Loon
  B. Log   **D.** Chair

0504. Carefully read the word pairs list in Fig. 9 aloud three times, then answer the question without referring back to the list. [STOP] Which of the following words rhymes with the word that was paired with "Folder"?

  A. Nearer   **C.** Men
  B. Sock   **D.** Chooser

MEMORY

0494–0504

123

FIGURE 10

PETAL ⟷ RING   TATTOO ⟷ STATUE
POT ⟷ TOY   LEGAL ⟷ HOOK
LEAD ⟷ WIG   MALL ⟷ FRUIT
BRAIN ⟷ SHOE   MILK ⟷ DREAM
NOSE ⟷ CANDLE   RICH ⟷ TISSUE

0505. Carefully read the word pairs list in Fig. 10 aloud three times, then answer the question without referring back to the list. [STOP] Which word was paired with "Brain"?

     A. Candle   **C.** Seam
     B. Wig   **D.** Shoe

0506. Carefully read the word pairs list in Fig. 10 aloud three times, then answer the question without referring back to the list. [STOP] Which of the following words rhymes with the word that was paired with "Lead"?

     A. Bog   **C.** Fig
     B. Boy   **D.** Few

0507. Carefully read the word pairs list in Fig. 10 aloud three times, then answer the question without referring back to the list. [STOP] Which of the following words rhymes with the word that was paired with "Mall"?

     A. Suit   **C.** Snapple
     B. Book   **D.** Seam

0508. Carefully read the word pairs list in Fig. 10 aloud three times, then answer the question without referring back to the list. [STOP] Which of the following words is most closely associated with the word that was paired with "Milk"?

     A. Food   **C.** Yard
     B. Sleep   **D.** Play

0509. Carefully read the word pairs list in Fig. 10 aloud three times, then answer the question without referring back to the list. [STOP] Which of the following words both have paired words that ended with "ue"?

     A. Tattoo; Closet   **C.** Rich; Nose
     B. Tattoo; Rich   **D.** Nose; Sand

FIGURE 11

JUICE ⟷ PALM	SAND ⟷ WHISTLE
PAINT ⟷ YAM	SHELL ⟷ MATCH
SHRUB ⟷ BRUSH	MAGNET ⟷ LAWN
CLIP ⟷ FOG	BRANCH ⟷ SEAM
WATER ⟷ SCREEN	CLOSET ⟷ APPLE

0510. Carefully read the word pairs list in Fig. 11 aloud three times, then answer the question without referring back to the list. [STOP] Which word was paired with "Paint"?

A. Palm
B. Ham
C. Ring
D. Yam

0511. Carefully read the word pairs list in Fig. 11 aloud three times, then answer the question without referring back to the list. [STOP] Which word was paired with "Shrub"?

A. Match
B. Whistle
C. Seam
D. Brush

0512. Carefully read the word pairs list in Fig. 11 aloud three times, then answer the question without referring back to the list. [STOP] Which of the following words is most closely associated with the word that was paired with "Clip"?

A. Tree
B. Clothes
C. Weather
D. Jewelry

0513. Carefully read the word pairs list in Fig. 11 aloud three times, then answer the question without referring back to the list. [STOP] Which of the following words has a paired word that spells a word both forward and backward?

A. Whistle
B. Branch
C. Seam
D. Paint

0514. Carefully read the word pairs list in Fig. 11 aloud three times, then answer the question without referring back to the list. [STOP] Which of the following words has a paired word that ends with "lm"?

A. Shrub
B. Sand
C. Juice
D. Branch

MEMORY

0505–0514

MENTAL FILES

Think about the most important files on your computer or in your filing cabinet. Do you have backups? If not, you probably would agree that you should back up your essential files and papers. This is also true of the most significant memories. We've discussed the various memory systems and how they operate independently. Take your most imperative memories and back them up through other memory systems. For example, it may be the combination to your home alarm or the combination to your safe. Encode this memory in both the verbal and visual memory systems. Picture yourself punching in the numbers on the keypad. Visualize where the numbers are in relation to each other or the pattern the combination creates on a keypad. The code is now backed up in visual memory. Now, for the next five times you enter in the combination, say the combination out loud as you enter it. This is adding a third backup system by utilizing the motor memory mechanisms of speech. By encoding the combination visually and motorically in addition to the traditional verbal rote memory, you create three separate backup memory systems, which are stored in three separate areas of your brain. You now have three separate routes (or neural pathways), thus increasing the efficiency with which you can later recall the memory. Try this in the next exercise by purposely making two distinct backups of the information presented to you.

FIGURE 12

0515. Emily Dickinson was what type of artist?

    A. Poet
    B. Non-fiction author
    C. Fiction writer
    D. Illustrator

0516. What is the value of pi?

    A. 3.14   **C.** 2.14
    B. 3.21   **D.** 3.41

0517. Which of the following famous classical composers composed *The Flower Waltz*?

    A. Johann Sebastian Bach
    B. Ludwig van Beethoven
    C. Pyotr Tchaikovsky
    D. Wolfgang Amadeus Mozart

0518. Without looking, what is the first name of the author of *Brain Boot Camp*?

    A. Mason   **C.** Douglas
    B. Davis   **D.** Dallas

ACRONYMS

Another memory strategy is the use of acronyms. Take Amber's schedule in Fig. 13, and turn it into an acronym. By taking the seven items from the schedule and creating a single word or phrase, you then only have one item to remember versus seven. For example:

A-lice
C-ar
R-oast
O-ptometrist
N-ancy
Y-oga
M-ike

FIGURE 13

AMBER'S SCHEDULE

8:00	Breakfast with Alice
9:00	Car to Mechanic
10:00	Place Roast in the Oven for Dinner
11:00	Appointment with Optometrist
12:00	Have Lunch with Nancy
1:00	Attend Yoga Class
2:00	Meet Mike at the Office

0519. You have thirty seconds to review Fig. 12 on p. 127. Press the ⟳ on the Coach, then answer the question as quickly as you can. [STOP] Which of the following hats was *not* included in the figure?

0520. You have thirty seconds to review Fig. 12 on p. 127. Press the ⟳ on the Coach, then answer the question as quickly as you can. [STOP] Which of the following hats was included in the figure?

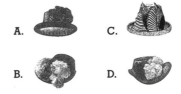

0521. You have thirty seconds to review Fig. 12 on p. 127. Press the ⟳ on the Coach, then answer the question as quickly as you can. [STOP] What is the hat shown at right missing compared to the one in Fig. 12?

  A. Feather
  B. Bow at back of hat
  C. Bow at bottom of strings
  D. Flower from bow

FIGURE 14

Dopey ←→ Apples
Grumpy ←→ Cantaloupe
Doc ←→ Carrots
Happy ←→ Tomatoes
Bashful ←→ Potatoes
Sleepy ←→ Oranges
Sneezy ←→ Cucumbers

0522. You have thirty seconds to review Fig. 12 on p. 127. Press the ⟳ on the Coach, then answer the question as quickly as you can. [STOP] How many total hats were pictured?

    A. Eleven   **C.** Nine
    B. Eight   **D.** Ten

0523. You have thirty seconds to review Fig. 12 on p. 127. Press the ⟳ on the Coach, then answer the question as quickly as you can. [STOP] Which object in the diagram was *not* within the hat category?

    A. Corset   **C.** Shoe
    B. Purse   **D.** Scarf

0524. You have thirty seconds to review Fig. 12 on p. 127. Press the ⟳ on the Coach, then answer the question as quickly as you can. [STOP] How many hats had feathers?

    A. Four   **C.** One
    B. Two   **D.** Three

0525. You have thirty seconds to review Fig. 12 on p. 127. Press the ⟳ on the Coach, then answer the question as quickly as you can. [STOP] How many hats had hanging ribbons?

    A. One   **C.** Two
    B. Four   **D.** Three

0526. In the periodic table, what does "Fe" stand for?

    A. Silver   **C.** Zinc
    B. Gold   **D.** Iron

0527. You have one minute to review Fig. 13 on p. 128. Press the ⏱ on the Coach, then answer the question as quickly as you can. [STOP] At what time was breakfast with Alice scheduled?

A. 7:00   C. 9:00

B. 10:00   D. 8:00

0528. You have one minute to review Fig. 13 on p. 128. Press the ⏱ on the Coach, then answer the question as quickly as you can. [STOP] At what time was Amber scheduled to take her car to the mechanic?

A. 8:00   C. 9:00

B. 11:00   D. 1:00

0529. You have one minute to review Fig. 13 on p. 128. Press the ⏱ on the Coach, then answer the question as quickly as you can. [STOP] At what time was Amber going to place the roast in the oven for dinner?

A. 1:00   C. 10:00

B. 8:00   D. 2:00

0530. You have one minute to review Fig. 13 on p. 128. Press the ⏱ on the Coach, then answer the question as quickly as you can. [STOP] When was Amber's appointment with the optometrist scheduled?

A. 2:00   C. 1:00

B. 12:00   D. 11:00

0531. You have one minute to review Fig. 13 on p. 128. Press the ⏱ on the Coach, then answer the question as quickly as you can. [STOP] At what time was lunch with Nancy?

A. 1:00   C. 12:00

B. 11:00   D. 2:00

0532. You have one minute to review Fig. 13 on p. 128. Press the ⏱ on the Coach, then answer the question as quickly as you can. [STOP] When was Amber going to attend yoga class?

A. 1:00   C. 8:00

B. 11:00   D. 10:00

0533. Without looking, what color is the diamond on the bottom of this page?

    A. Blue   **C.** Green
    B. Red   **D.** Yellow

0534. You have one minute to review Fig. 13 on p. 128. Press the ↻ on the Coach, then answer the question as quickly as you can. [STOP] When was Amber going to meet Mike at the office?

    A. 12:00   **C.** 10:00
    B. 9:00   **D.** 2:00

0535. Carefully read the word pairs list in Fig. 14 on p. 129 aloud three times, then answer the question without referring back to the list. [STOP] Which item was Happy associated with?

    A. Apples   **C.** Tomatoes
    B. Potatoes   **D.** Oranges

0536. Carefully read the word pairs list in Fig. 14 on p. 129 aloud three times, then answer the question without referring back to the list. [STOP] Which fruit should be associated with Doc, but isn't?

    A. Apples   **C.** Tomatoes
    B. Carrots   **D.** Oranges

0537. Carefully read the word pairs list in Fig. 14 on p. 129 aloud three times, then answer the question without referring back to the list. [STOP] Which dwarfs were associated with things you would use in a salad?

    A. Doc, Happy, Sneezy
    B. Doc, Dopey, Sleepy
    C. Doc, Sleepy, Sneezy
    D. Doc, Grumpy, Happy

0538. Carefully read the word pairs list in Fig. 14 on p. 129 aloud three times, then answer the question without referring back to the list. [STOP] Which dwarfs were associated with traditional fruit?

    A. Doc, Dopey, Sleepy
    B. Doc, Sneezy, Bashful
    C. Dopey, Grumpy, Sleepy
    D. Dopey, Grumpy, Sleepy, Sneezy

MEMORY

0527–0538

ELABORATION IMPROVES MEMORY

Did you find that for Fig. 15 it was easier to remember the spaghetti sauce, the cake mix, and the lightbulbs? This is because the more detail you associate with an object, the better the quality of the memory created. The thought of a dog eating a dish sponge or using spaghetti sauce to frost the daughter's cake is the type of detail that is difficult to forget. Another factor at play is what is called *primacy* and *recency* effects. These effects refer to our tendency to remember items at the beginning and at the end of a list. So, if you have a list, place the most important items at the front or back and don't forget to elaborate by adding details.

FIGURE 15

John has to finish his shopping this afternoon. He is well acquainted with his local grocery store and organizes his grocery list according to location. In Aisle 1 he has to remember to get apples. In Aisle 2 he will pick up bread. In Aisle 3 he has to get the cake mix so he can bake a cake in celebration for his daughter's third birthday. As he passes through the 4th Aisle, he will pick up a can of chicken noodle soup, and in Aisle 5 he will need to remember to get a dish sponge to replace the one that his dog ate. Finally, in the 6th Aisle he has to get the spaghetti sauce to place on his daughter's cake.

0539. Review the list in Fig. 14 on p. 129 carefully, then answer the question without referring back to the list. [STOP] Which of the following food items was *not* listed?

    A. Grapes   **C.** Cucumbers
    B. Carrots   **D.** Potatoes

0540. Review the list in Fig. 14 on p. 129 carefully, then answer the question without referring back to the list. [STOP] If you wanted to make a salad with the listed items and then realized you also needed lettuce, what would be a good way to remember the lettuce?

    A. Forget it   **C.** Memorize it
    B. Repetition   **D.** Associate with Snow White

0541. Read Fig. 15, and try to remember the items John must get at the grocery store; then answer the question without referring back to the story. [STOP] What does John need to get from Aisle 1?

    A. Cake mix
    B. Chicken noodle soup
    C. Apples
    D. Bread

0542. Read Fig. 15, and try to remember the items John must get at the grocery store; then answer the question without referring back to the story. [STOP] Where will John find bread?

    A. Aisle 3   **C.** Aisle 1
    B. Aisle 2   **D.** Aisle 5

FIGURE 16

0543. Read Fig. 15, and try to remember the items John must get at the grocery store; then answer the question without referring back to the story. [STOP] What does John need to get from Aisle 3?

    A. Cake mix   **C.** Dish sponge
    B. Apples   **D.** Chicken noodle soup

0544. Read Fig. 15, and try to remember the items John must get at the grocery store; then answer the question without referring back to the story. [STOP] Where will John find chicken noodle soup?

    A. Aisle 5   **C.** Aisle 6
    B. Aisle 3   **D.** Aisle 4

0545. Read Fig. 15, and try to remember the items John must get at the grocery store; then answer the question without referring back to the story. [STOP] What does John need to get from Aisle 5?

    A. Cake mix   **C.** Spaghetti sauce
    B. Dish sponge   **D.** Bread

0546. Read Fig. 15, and try to remember the items John must get at the grocery store; then answer the question without referring back to the story. [STOP] What does John need to get from Aisle 6?

    A. Cake mix   **C.** Chicken noodle soup
    B. Apples   **D.** Spaghetti sauce

0547. You have thirty seconds to review Fig. 16 on p. 133. Press the ⏱ on the Coach, then answer the question as quickly as you can. [STOP] How many of the shoes were ankle boots?

    A. Six   **C.** Seven
    B. Five   **D.** Eight

0548. You have thirty seconds to review Fig. 16 on p. 133. Press the ⏱ on the Coach, then answer the question as quickly as you can. [STOP] Which of the following shoes was *not* shown?

    A.   **C.**

    B.   **D.**

0549. You have thirty seconds to review Fig. 16 on p. 133. Press the ⏱ on the Coach, then answer the question as quickly as you can. [STOP] In which row was the shoe shown at right?

    A. Row 3   **C.** Row 2
    B. Row 4   **D.** Row 1

0550. You have thirty seconds to review Fig. 16 on p. 133. Press the ⏱ on the Coach, then answer the question as quickly as you can. [STOP] How many shoes were open-toe?

    A. Two   **C.** One
    B. Three   **D.** None

0551. You have thirty seconds to review Fig. 16 on p. 133. Press the ⏱ on the Coach, then answer the question as quickly as you can. [STOP] Which of the following shoes was *not* shown?

    A.   **C.**

    B.   **D.**

0552. You have thirty seconds to review Fig. 16 on p. 133. Press the ↻ on the Coach, then answer the question as quickly as you can. [STOP] How many total shoes were shown?

    A. Twenty   **C.** Twenty-four
    B. Twenty-one **D.** Twenty-two

0553. You have thirty seconds to review Fig. 16 on p. 133. Press the ↻ on the Coach, then answer the question as quickly as you can. [STOP] In which row was the shoe shown at right?

    A. Row 2   **C.** Row 1
    B. Row 3   **D.** Row 4

0554. You have thirty seconds to review Fig. 16 on p. 133. Press the ↻ on the Coach, then answer the question as quickly as you can. [STOP] Which of the following shoes was *not* shown?

    A.   **C.**

    B.   **D.**

0555. You have thirty seconds to review Fig. 16 on p. 133. Press the ↻ on the Coach, then answer the question as quickly as you can. [STOP] How many pairs of shoes were displayed on a pillow?

    A. One   **C.** Three
    B. Two   **D.** None

0556. You have thirty seconds to review Fig. 16 on p. 133. Press the ↻ on the Coach, then answer the question as quickly as you can. [STOP] How many shoes had buckles?

    A. Two   **C.** Three
    B. None   **D.** One

RELAX ...
TO REMEMBER

Have you ever noticed that when you are busy running around and have a wide array of things on your mind, or are in the midst of a period of high stress, that your memory tends to "slip" more frequently? During these times, our attention is divided. Our autonomic nervous system is activated (the "fight or flight" response), thus shutting down higher-order functions, such as attention or memory. It is nearly impossible to encode new information when we are not paying attention. So, take a breath, relax both your mind and body, and focus on whatever you need to absorb. You may be surprised how much more efficiently your mind works when you allow yourself to slow down and relax.

FIGURE 17

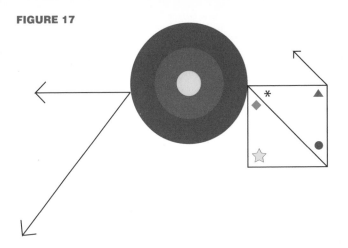

0557. You have thirty seconds to review Fig. 16 on p. 133. Press the ⏱ on the Coach, then answer the question as quickly as you can. [STOP] Which of the following shoes was shown?

A.   C.

B.   D.

0558. You have thirty seconds to review Fig. 16 on p. 133. Press the ⏱ on the Coach, then answer the question as quickly as you can. [STOP] How many shoes were flat, with no heel?

   A. Three   **C.** Two
   B. Four   **D.** Five

0559. What is Earth's largest continent?

   A. North America **C.** Europe
   B. Africa   **D.** Asia

0560. In which year was the compact disc introduced?

   A. 1974   **C.** 1980
   B. 1983   **D.** 1960

On a separate sheet of paper, draw Fig. 18 from memory. After the drawing is complete, go back and compare your drawing to the original figure. Are the two similar? If you were able to draw at least half of the figure correctly, then you are doing very well!

0561. You have thirty seconds to review Fig. 17 on p. 137. Press the ⏱ on the Coach, then answer the question as quickly as you can. [STOP] How many arrows were in the drawing?

A. One **C.** Three
B. Two **D.** Four

0562. You have thirty seconds to review Fig. 17 on p. 137. Press the ⏱ on the Coach, then answer the question as quickly as you can. [STOP] What was the color of the smallest circle?

A. Yellow **C.** Green
B. Blue **D.** Red

0563. You have thirty seconds to review Fig. 17 on p. 137. Press the ⏱ on the Coach, then answer the question as quickly as you can. [STOP] Which shape was blue?

A. Triangle **C.** Star
B. Diamond **D.** Small circle

0564. You have thirty seconds to review Fig. 17 on p. 137. Press the ⏱ on the Coach, then answer the question as quickly as you can. [STOP] Which of the following shapes was *not* in the diagram?

A. Pentagon **C.** Diamond
B. Circle **D.** Square

0565. Review Fig. 17 on p. 137, then think of ten words that begin with the letter "P" before answering the question. [STOP] Which of the following correctly depicts the square in the figure?

A.   **C.**

B.   **D.**

FIGURE 18

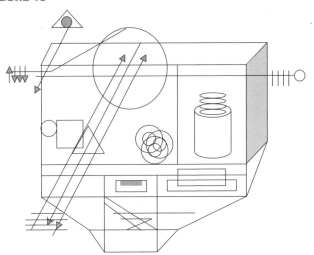

0566. Review Fig. 17 on p. 137, then count by 3s to 33 before answering the question. [STOP] Which of the following correctly depicts the circle portion from the figure?

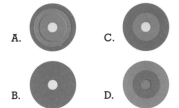

A.

B.

C.

D.

0567. Review Fig. 17 on p. 137, then say the alphabet backwards before answering the question. [STOP] What color was the diamond?

    A. Blue   **C.** Yellow
    B. Red   **D.** Green

0568. Review Fig. 17 on p. 137, then read the sidebar on p. 132 before answering the question. [STOP] What color was the rectangle?

    A. Green   **C.** Blue
    B. Red   **D.** There was no rectangle

MEMORY

0561–
0568

139

Calming the brain is an essential part of good memory. For example, closing your eyes even for a few moments will conserve mental energy and limit distractions. Also, the color blue is known to calm the brain. So if you are trying to remember something or want to enhance encoding, a trick you can do is to close your eyes just for a moment and imagine the color blue.

0569. You have one minute to review Fig. 18 on p. 139. Press the ⟳ on the Coach, then answer the question as quickly as you can. [STOP] Which of the following figures was part of Fig. 18?

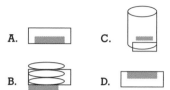

0570. You have one minute to review Fig. 18 on p. 139. Press the ⟳ on the Coach, then answer the question as quickly as you can. [STOP] In the upper right region of the figure, the large line below had several other lines bisecting it. How many small lines were bisecting the larger line?

A. Six   **C.** Five
B. Three   **D.** Four

0571. You have one minute to review Fig. 18 on p. 139. Press the ⟳ on the Coach, then answer the question as quickly as you can. [STOP] On which side of the page did the figure from question no. 570 appear?

    A. Lower portion of the page
    B. Upper portion of the page

0572. You have one minute to review Fig. 18 on p. 139. Press the ⟳ on the Coach, then answer the question as quickly as you can. [STOP] Which of the following figures was part of Fig. 18?

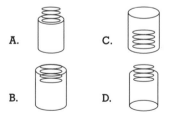

0573. You have one minute to review Fig. 18 on p. 139. Press the ⟳ on the Coach, then answer the question as quickly as you can. [STOP] On which side of the figure did the diagram shown at right appear?

    A. Left side of page
    B. Right side of the page

0574. You have one minute to review Fig. 18 on p. 139. Press the ⟳ on the Coach, then answer the question as quickly as you can. [STOP] How many of the individual figures were shaded in Fig. 18?

    A. Five   **C.** Three
    B. Four   **D.** Two

0575. You have one minute to review Fig. 18 on p. 139. Press the ⟳ on the Coach, then answer the question as quickly as you can. [STOP] Which of the following figures was part of Fig. 18?

    A.   **C.**

    B.   **D.**

0576. You have one minute to review Fig. 18 on p. 139. Press the ⟳ on the Coach, then answer the question as quickly as you can. [STOP] Which of the following figures was part of Fig. 18?

    A.   **C.**

    B.   **D.**

0577. How long is the term for the president of the United States?

    A. Four months   **C.** Five years
    B. Four years   **D.** Eight years

MEMORY

0569–0577

FIGURE 19

Carol asked her husband, Carl, to run a few errands on his way home from the Country Club. Carol had finally completed her menu for the evening and decided to serve asparagus as the vegetable instead of cauliflower. Carol, a connoisseur of fine wine, requested Carl select a nice red Chianti from the local liquor store. She also asked Carl to go to the grocery store and purchase 2 loaves of French bread, 4 Cornish hens, fresh asparagus, heavy whipping cream, coffee creamer, and cream cheese. Carl completed a round of golf, beating his long-standing personal record at the Palisades. His new record was 3 points over the 18-hole par of 72. Carl could hardly wait to brag to his brother Kent and his Army buddy, Cartwright. Now those guys could golf; his brother's best score was 80 and Cartwright's personal best was 78. When Carl arrived at the grocery store, he headed to the wine section, selected a nice Cabernet Sauvignon he knew his wife would love, 2 Cornish hens, 2 loaves of French bread, whipping cream, cream cheese, and coffee creamer. This was going to be a great dinner with Cartwright and Cathryn.

0578. Read Fig. 19, then answer the question without referring back to the story. [STOP] Which of the following items did Carl forget to purchase at the grocery store?

    A. Green beans   **C.** Asparagus
    B. Cauliflower   **D.** Broccoli

0579. Read Fig. 19, then answer the question without referring back to the story. [STOP] How many Cornish hens was Carl supposed to buy?

    A. 4   **C.** 3
    B. 2   **D.** 5

0580. Read Fig. 19, then answer the question without referring back to the story. [STOP] What was Carl's new golf record?

    A. 80   **C.** 75
    B. 72   **D.** 78

0581. Read Fig. 19, then answer the question without referring back to the story. [STOP] What was Carl's brother's first name?

    A. Cartwright   **C.** Kent
    B. Ken   **D.** Kevin

0582. Read Fig. 19, then answer the question without referring back to the story. [STOP] What kind of wine was Carl supposed to buy?

    A. Côtes du Rhône
    B. Cabernet Sauvignon
    C. Cabernet Franc
    D. Chianti

0583. Read Fig. 19, then answer the question without referring back to the story. [STOP] What was the name of the golf course?

    A. Park Place   **C.** Pebble Beach
    B. Palace Place   **D.** Palisades

0584. Read Fig. 19, then answer the question without referring back to the story. [STOP] What vegetable had Carol considered serving?

    A. Corn   **C.** Cauliflower
    B. Broccoli   **D.** Kale

0585. Read Fig. 19, then answer the question without referring back to the story. [STOP] Which item did Carl buy incorrectly?

    A. Cream cheese
    B. Whipping cream
    C. Coffee creamer
    D. Ice cream

0586. Read Fig. 19, then answer the question without referring back to the story. [STOP] What was Carl's wife's name?

    A. Caty   **C.** Carolyn
    B. Carol   **D.** Cathryn

0587. Read Fig. 19, then answer the question without referring back to the story. [STOP] What was Cartwright's personal best on the golf course?

    A. 78   **C.** 80
    B. 76   **D.** 75

MEMORY

0578–0587

143

FIGURE 20

	1	2	3	4	5	6	7
1	H	♥	■	M	■	♥	T
2	●	Q	5	O	A	Q	■
3	▲	♣	L	T	M	♣	●
4	F	A	T	H	E	R	S
5	▲	♣	M	E	L	♣	●
6	●	Q	A	R	A	Q	■
7	H	♦	♠	S	♠	♦	T

0588. You have fifteen seconds to review Fig. 20. Press the ⏱ on the Coach, then answer the question as quickly as you can without referring back to the figure. [STOP] What letters were in the corners of the grid?

    A. Q and T   **C.** W and H
    B. H and T   **D.** T and S

0589. You have fifteen seconds to review Fig. 20. Press the ⏱ on the Coach, then answer the question as quickly as you can without referring back to the figure. [STOP] Which number was shown in the grid?

    A. 5   **C.** 6
    B. 2   **D.** 8

0590. You have fifteen seconds to review Fig. 20. Press the ⏱ on the Coach, then answer the question as quickly as you can without referring back to the figure. [STOP] What word was shown vertically on the grid?

    A. FEATHERS   **C.** FATHERS
    B. MOWERS   **D.** MOTHERS

0591. What is the most common blood type?

    A. A   **C.** O
    B. B   **D.** B+

144

FIGURE 21

	1	2	3	4	5
1	R	□	◇	□	●
2	□	A	♥	A	◇
3	◇	♥	W	♥	□
4	□	A	♥	A	◇
5	●	◇	□	◇	R

0592. You have fifteen seconds to review Fig. 21. Press the ⏱ on the Coach, then answer the question as quickly as you can without referring back to the figure. [STOP] What letter was in two corners of the grid?

    A. R   **C.** A
    B. W   **D.** S

0593. You have fifteen seconds to review Fig. 21. Press the ⏱ on the Coach, then answer the question as quickly as you can without referring back to the figure. [STOP] What shape was in two corners of the grid?

    A. ♥   **C.** ●
    B. Square **D.** Diamond

0594. You have fifteen seconds to review Fig. 21. Press the ⏱ on the Coach, then answer the question as quickly as you can without referring back to the figure. [STOP] What was in the center of the grid?

    A. W   **C.** ♥
    B. ●   **D.** □

0595. You have fifteen seconds to review Fig. 21. Press the ⏱ on the Coach, then answer the question as quickly as you can without referring back to the figure. [STOP] Which shape or letter was *not* included in the grid?

    A. ◇   **C.** A
    B. □   **D.** S

MEMORY ASSOCIATION

Memory in the brain works through association. The concept of an apple is stored next to other fruits and other items that are round and red and other items that are sweet. You can use this to your advantage. If you have to remember something quickly and effectively, just piggyback it onto an existing memory. For example, maybe you need to remember the name of a new cereal that you want to try. The cereal's name is Cornergy. By piggybacking Cornergy onto an existing cereal, Corn Flakes®, you don't need to memorize a new name. Remember, the more purposeful the strategy used in encoding, the less effort will be needed in retrieval.

FIGURE 22

	1	2	3
1	▲	♥	▲
2	■	●	■
3	▲	♥	▲

0596. You have fifteen seconds to review Fig. 22. Press the ⏱ on the Coach, then answer the question as quickly as you can without referring back to the figure. [STOP] What shape was in each corner?

    A. Squares   **C.** Triangles
    B. Circles   **D.** Diamonds

0597. You have fifteen seconds to review Fig. 22. Press the ⏱ on the Coach, then answer the question as quickly as you can without referring back to the figure. [STOP] Which shape was in the center of the grid?

    A. Oval   **C.** Diamond
    B. Circle   **D.** Heart

0598. You have fifteen seconds to review Fig. 22. Press the ⏱ on the Coach, then answer the question as quickly as you can without referring back to the figure. [STOP] Which shape was *not* included in the grid?

    A. Diamond   **C.** Triangle
    B. Heart   **D.** Square

0599. Without looking, which direction is the butterfly on this page facing?

    A. Facing up   **C.** Facing left
    B. Facing right   **D.** Facing down

0600. What is the sign for bass clef?

    A. ♪   **C.** 𝄞

    B. ♫   **D.** 𝄢

MEMORY

0596–0600

147

LANGUAGE

EXPRESSIVE & RECEPTIVE

Language is part of our everyday world and is the key to interacting with others. Central to communication, language is a very complex function, generally located in the temporal lobes, and is a complex symbolic representation of our inner and outer worlds as well as the system for employing these representations.

Expressive language is the ability to express oneself and includes converting our thoughts to words, word finding, and the flow of words. Receptive language is the ability to understand others and encompasses hearing and understanding spoken language.

Portions of spoken language that consist of tone, sequencing, and rhythm are typically processed on the right side of the brain. Articulation and individual components of speech, such as letters, words, and sentence structure, are usually processed on the left side of the brain. Each side of the brain must communicate back and forth in rapid succession in order to process and integrate the various components of language.

It is important to note that the spoken word has come along relatively late in our evolution. More primitive forms of communication, such as tone and nonverbal gesturing, are wired deeper into the brain, meaning they have more impact on the recipient than spoken words. For example, answering a question from your spouse or sibling with a verbal yes but shaking your head no sends a mixed message. The nonverbal gesture registers stronger with your wife or brother than your spoken word. Try saying "yes" and shaking your head no. It's difficult! Similarly, tone is also a more primitive function of language, and thus it takes precedence over the spoken word. As another example, if you tell your friend that you like her shoes, but use a tone that contradicts the words, the tone will be registered over the words.

Language is so vast and so complex that it is quite difficult to isolate it to a single area of the brain. Because of this complexity, it is also challenging to identify which aspects may not be functioning at full capacity. Therefore, the best way to improve your language is through practice. Read challenging material on a topic of interest. Focus on the challenging words, and make an effort to comprehend the material. Learn new vocabulary words, and use them in daily conversation. And vary the material, for the greatest flexibility in your language capacity.

Within this chapter, we focus on Expressive language by quizzing you on vocabulary words, common and not-common expressions, and a variety of other challenges involving the use of words. These exercises are designed to stretch your brain, not only improving word usage but also your creativity by having your mind think in abstract ways. Through these exercises, your overall language capability will improve as the brain forms new connections and strengthens existing ones.

0601. You have two minutes to use the letters below to create words, using each letter only once. Press the ⏱ on the Coach, then complete the task as quickly as you can. How many words did you create?

KDSFJGHWEIRHFCVJZCJAEFIUD

A. More than 20   C. 11–15
B. 16–20   D. 10 or less

0602. What is the meaning of the word "malingering"?

A. Being sick
B. Exaggerating illness
C. Violent
D. Hypochondriac

0603. What is the meaning of the word "altruistic"?

A. Selfless concern for others
B. Independent
C. Truthful
D. Selfish

0604. What is the meaning of the word "encryption"?

A. Egyptian writing
B. Concealed information
C. To send out information
D. A coffin

0605. What is the meaning of the word "anhedonia"?

A. Pleasurable acts
B. Depression
C. Unable to experience pleasure
D. An animal

FIGURE 1

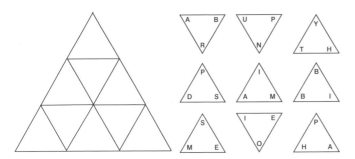

0606. Using Fig. 1, arrange the triangles into a pyramid to spell increasingly longer words. You will spell one-, two-, four-, five-, seven-, and eight-letter words. What four-letter word can you spell within the pyramid?

    A. Some   **C.** Hand
    B. Puppy   **D.** Baby

0607. Using Fig. 1, arrange the triangles into a pyramid to spell increasingly longer words. You will spell one-, two-, four-, five-, seven-, and eight-letter words. Which triangle goes at the top of the pyramid?

    A. PHA   **C.** IAM
    B. UPN   **D.** SME

0608. Using Fig. 1, arrange the triangles into a pyramid to spell increasingly longer words. You will spell one-, two-, four-, five-, seven-, and eight-letter words. Which triangle is the bottom right corner of the pyramid?

    A. PHA   **C.** SME
    B. ABR   **D.** YTH

0609. Using Fig. 1, arrange the triangles into a pyramid to spell increasingly longer words. You will spell one-, two-, four-, five-, seven-, and eight-letter words. Which triangles work together to make up a five-letter word within the pyramid?

    A. BBI, IEO, YTH   **C.** PDS, IEO, SME
    B. UPN, PDS, ITO   **D.** BBI, ABR, YTH

FIGURE 2

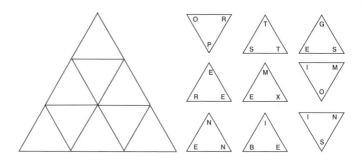

0610. Using Fig. 2, arrange the triangles into a pyramid to spell increasingly longer words. You will spell one-, two-, four-, five-, seven-, and eight-letter words. What four-letter word can you spell within the pyramid?

    A. Time   **C.** Ring
    B. Morn   **D.** Tore

0611. Using Fig. 2, arrange the triangles into a pyramid to spell increasingly longer words. You will spell one-, two-, four-, five-, seven-, and eight-letter words. Which triangle goes at the top of the pyramid?

    A. TST   **C.** GES
    B. ERE   **D.** IBE

0612. Using Fig. 2, arrange the triangles into a pyramid to spell increasingly longer words. You will spell one-, two-, four-, five-, seven-, and eight-letter words. Which triangle is the bottom right corner of the pyramid?

    A. GES   **C.** NEN
    B. TST   **D.** MEX

0613. Using Fig. 2, arrange the triangles into a pyramid to spell increasingly longer words. You will spell one-, two-, four-, five-, seven-, and eight-letter words. Which triangles work together to make up a five-letter word within the pyramid?

    A. ORP, INS, ERE   **C.** TST, IBE, GES
    B. TST, IMO, ERE **D.** TST, IMO, NEN

0614. Which letter is missing from the scrambled word below?

SYEMRT

A. Y   **C.** I
B. T   **D.** S

0615. Which letter is missing from the scrambled word below?

LCRETIYICT

A. A   **C.** E
B. V   **D.** R

0616. Which letter is missing from the scrambled word below?

MANHTO

A. E   **C.** R
B. S   **D.** P

0617. You have two minutes to use the letters below to create words, using each letter only once. Press the ⏻ on the Coach, then complete the task as quickly as you can. How many words did you create?

A. More than 25   **C.** 11–17
B. 18–24   **D.** 10 or less

0618. What is the picture below of?

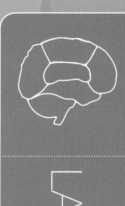

A. Rose   **C.** Carnation
B. Petunia   **D.** Zinnia

VOCABULARY

Vocabulary is one of the few skill sets that actually improves with age. It is also the primary cognitive function that stays with us the longest. We've included quite a few vocabulary words in this book to help facilitate your brain growth. Begin using these words in your everyday conversations, and continue to develop your brain by reading materials that further develop your vocabulary.

0619. Which letter is missing from the scrambled word below?

GEIGN

A. O   C. R
B. F   D. P

0620. Which letter is missing from the scrambled word below?

NERIGO

A. V   C. S
B. G   D. F

0621. What is the meaning of the word "ocular"?

A. About the ear   C. Oval shaped
B. About the eye   D. Glasses

0622. I am the fifth letter in adam_nt and the seventh letter in mendic_nt. What letter am I? Hint: I'm so confused. Now would that be like adherent or indignant?

A. E   C. I
B. A   D. U

0623. Select the best word to complete the sentence below.

Please _____ my apology.

A. Except
B. Accept

0624. Select the best word to complete the sentence below.

She seemed very _____.

A. Confident
B. Confidant

Solve the cryptogram below by deciphering the phrase, substituting letters for numbers. Under what category does the answer fit?

A	B	C	D	E	F	G	H	I	J	K	L	M
					11							

N	O	P	Q	R	S	T	U	V	W	X	Y	Z
		19					5					

$$\overline{5}\ \overline{19}\quad \overline{21}\ \overline{4}\qquad \overline{8}\ \overline{12}\ \overline{5}\ \overset{F}{\overline{11}}\ \overset{F}{\overline{11}}$$

A. Country   **C.** Phrase
B. Holiday   **D.** Food

0626. What is the meaning of the word "apropos"?

    A. Boredom
    B. To know the latest information
    C. A fixed idea
    D. Appropriate for the situation

0627. Under which category does the scrambled word below fall?

SSPUGARAA

    A. Fruit   **C.** Vegetable
    B. Animal   **D.** City

0628. What is the meaning of the word "insurrection"?

    A. An intersection   **C.** A violent uprising
    B. A resurrection   **D.** An insertion

0629. I am the sixth letter in maint_nance and the fourth letter in rel_vant. What letter am I?

    A. E   **C.** I
    B. A   **D.** O

LANGUAGE

0619–
0629

0630. Which letter is missing from the scrambled word below?

KUEYR

A. H   **C.** L
B. M   **D.** T

0631. Under which category does the scrambled word below fall?

MASTORAENC

A. Fruit   **C.** Vegetable
B. City   **D.** Animal

0632. What is the meaning of the word "bureaucracy"?

A. Managed government
B. Anarchy
C. Monarchy
D. President

0633. What is the meaning of the word "pervasive"?

A. Localized   **C.** Secular
B. Global   **D.** Widespread

0634. Select the best word to complete the sentence below.

She had to _____ her dress.

A. Pin
B. Pen

0635. What is the meaning of the word "prominent"?

A. To promote   **C.** To dance
B. Standing out   **D.** To produce

0636. Solve the cryptogram below by deciphering the phrase, substituting numbers for letters. Under what category does the answer fit?

A	B	C	D	E	F	G	H	I	J	K	L	M
	17										23	

N	O	P	Q	R	S	T	U	V	W	X	Y	Z
					13							

$$\underset{13}{\text{S}}\ \underset{24}{—}\ \underset{12}{—}\ \underset{23}{—}\ \underset{23}{—} \qquad \underset{22}{—}\ \underset{6}{—}\ \underset{1}{—} \qquad \underset{17}{\text{B}}\ \underset{1}{—}\ \underset{18}{—}\ \underset{5}{—}\ \underset{13}{\text{S}}$$

- **A.** City
- **C.** Phrase
- **B.** Song
- **D.** Movie

0637. What is the meaning of the word "artisan"?

- **A.** Baker
- **C.** Craftsman
- **B.** Painter
- **D.** Gallery

0638. I am the fourth letter in lia_son and the third letter in le_sure. What letter am I?

- **A.** Y
- **C.** I
- **B.** E
- **D.** A

0639. What does the puzzle below represent?

$$\frac{\text{ATTEN}}{\text{TION}}$$

- **A.** Attention matters
- **B.** Center of attention
- **C.** Divided attention
- **D.** Not paying attention

0640. What is the nine-letter word referenced in this book to describe self-knowledge of deficits? Hint: There are several pairs in me.

- **A.** Awareness
- **C.** Cognizant
- **B.** Knowledge
- **D.** Diagnosed

FIGURE 3

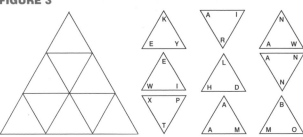

0641. Using Fig. 3, arrange the triangles into a pyramid to spell increasingly longer words. You will spell one-, two-, four-, five-, seven-, and eight-letter words. What is a four-letter word within the pyramid?

    A. Draw   **C.** Bank

    B. With   **D.** More

0642. Using Fig. 3, arrange the triangles into a pyramid to spell increasingly longer words. You will spell one-, two-, four-, five-, seven-, and eight-letter words. Which triangle goes at the top of the pyramid?

    A. AAM   **C.** BMO

    B. KEY   **D.** LHD

0643. Using Fig. 3, arrange the triangles into a pyramid to spell increasingly longer words. You will spell one-, two-, four-, five-, seven-, and eight-letter words. Which triangle is in the bottom right corner of the pyramid?

    A. NAW   **C.** EWI

    B. ANN   **D.** AAM

0644. Using Fig. 3, arrange the triangles into a pyramid to spell increasingly longer words. You will spell one, two-, four-, five-, seven-, and eight-letter words. Which triangles work together to make up a five-letter word within the triangle?

    A. BMO, ANN, KEY

    B. XPT, AIR, NAW

    C. BMO, AIR, KEY

    D. BMO, AAM, KEY

0645. I am the fifth letter in disp_rate and the fourth letter in sep_rate, and neither word describes a person whom we should venerate. What letter am I?

    A. E   **C.** I
    B. A   **D.** U

0646. You have two minutes to use the letters below to create words, using each letter only once. Press the ⏱ on the Coach, then complete the task as quickly as you can. How many words did you create?

ADHISDFKEHCHIADLAJIEHALSKDFHEH

    A. More than 15   **C.** 9–11
    B. 12–15   **D.** Less than 9

0647. What is the meaning of the word "chivalry"?

    A. Charity   **C.** Unraveled
    B. Diversity   **D.** Honor code

0648. What is the meaning of the word "manifestation"?

    A. Festival
    B. Manipulation
    C. Materialization
    D. Chauvinist

0649. Pearl is to Sand as Diamond is to _____?

    A. Coal   **C.** Mine
    B. Mineral   **D.** Ring

0650. Yeast is to Bread as _____ is to Cost?

    A. Price   **C.** Inflation
    B. Labor   **D.** Material

LANGUAGE

0641–
0650

FIGHT OR FLIGHT

When we are anxious, our minds and bodies launch into fight-or-flight mode. This represents the activation of the autonomic nervous system, which has allowed us to survive as a species for millions of years. This group of psychological and physiological responses shut down memory, attention, language, and other cognitive functions—in order to focus on staying alive in a crisis. Fight-or-flight mode will get you out of the way of an oncoming truck, but if used frequently over a long period of time, it can begin to destroy higher cognitive functions. Our modern version of fight-or-flight mode is anxiety and stress, and we must actively counter both to keep our minds effective and efficient. This can be done through diet, nutrition, exercise, active relaxation exercises, meditation, and just plain fun. Sometimes our anxiety can be self-induced by making a mountain out of the proverbial molehill. We must train ourselves to keep stress in perspective, or else it can take over our ability to function, both mentally and physically.

0651. What is the meaning of the word "foray"?

    A. To be fortunate
    B. Fortify
    C. To make a brief excursion
    D. Deplore

0652. What does the puzzle below represent?

IN
MYHEAD

    A. It's raining in my head
    B. In over my head
    C. Can't get it out of my head
    D. In and around my head

0653. What is the meaning of the word "impulsive"?

    A. Thoughtful
    B. Implication
    C. Pulse rate
    D. Acting without thought

0654. Select the best word to complete the sentence below.

Mrs. Jones made a good _____.

    A. Principal
    B. Principle

0655. Select the best word to complete the sentence below.

His dastardly deeds made him _____.

    A. Famous
    B. Infamous

0656. What is the meaning of the word "brandish"?

    A. Show off   **C.** Discreet
    B. Victorious   **D.** Humble

0657. Solve the cryptogram below by deciphering the phrase, substituting numbers for letters. Under what category does the answer fit?

A	B	C	D	E	F	G	H	I	J	K	L	M
											15	

N	O	P	Q	R	S	T	U	V	W	X	Y	Z
9				19		5						

```
__  __  __    __  O   __  __  O   __    __  O   __  __  __  R
5   14  4     23  9   5   5   9   21    13  9   15  15  17  19
```

A. Movie   **C.** Song
B. Event   **D.** Phrase

0658. You have two minutes to use the letters below to create words, using each letter only once. Press the ⏱ on the Coach, then complete the task as quickly as you can. How many words did you create?

a i e j e k f k h d s a k n c

A. More than 15   **C.** 9–12
B. 12–15   **D.** Less than 9

0659. Which letter is missing from the scrambled word below?

DASEYTRE

A. Y   **C.** N
B. Z   **D.** U

0660. What is the meaning of the word "rapacious"?

A. Greedy   **C.** Repetitive
B. Generous   **D.** Mean

0661. Find the eight-letter world in the grid below by moving both horizontally and vertically. Under what category does the word fit?

B	R	I	E	P
E	V	D	G	W
J	I	L	L	B
S	U	C	A	S
W	O	R	G	E

A. Wedding **C.** Water
B. Settlement **D.** Reef

0662. I am the third letter in ab_ence, the sixth letter in super_ede. What letter am I? Hint: Don't let any one try to deceive you.

A. Z **C.** S
B. C **D.** G

0663. What does the term "bona fides" mean?

A. Up-to-date
B. The matter at hand
C. Proof of credentials
D. A football fan

0664. What does the phrase "A rising tide lifts all boats" mean?

A. A storm will create flooding
B. A tide will cause the boats to come ashore
C. An ambitious person will be more successful than a person who does not try to achieve anything
D. A strong economy will lift spirits

0665. What is the meaning of the word "instigate"?

A. Provoke **C.** Instinct
B. Investigate **D.** Instant replay

LANGUAGE

0657–
0665

0666. Solve the cryptogram below by deciphering the phrase, substituting numbers for letters. Under what category does the answer fit?

A	B	C	D	E	F	G	H	I	J	K	L	M
	17											

N	O	P	Q	R	S	T	U	V	W	X	Y	Z
	11			8								

17 8 12 9 21 1   11 20 1 8

22 8 11 3 17 23 1 9   15 18 22 1 8

A. Movie   **C.** Song
B. Phrase   **D.** Quote

0667. What is the meaning of the word "ramification"?

A. An action   **C.** Punishment
B. A thought   **D.** Consequence

0668. Which letter is missing from the scrambled word below?

ANPEAC

A. O   **C.** R
B. K   **D.** S

0669. Which letter is missing from the scrambled word below?

NLARACI

A. T   **C.** C
B. V   **D.** E

0670. Which letter is missing from the scrambled word below?

RLVTOEA

A. C   **C.** Y
B. D   **D.** E

FIGURE 4

G	S	B	E	A	N	T
R	E	T	O	H	N	K
O	I	T	R	A	Y	A
U	E	C	T	O	T	E
N	I	S	E	A	N	W
D	N	O	O	Q	L	G
I	B	R	E	W	E	D

NOTE: Words can be found horizontally, vertically, and diagonally. Do *not* count variations of words (e.g., if you find "walk" and "walked," you may only count "walked" as one word).

0671. Using Fig. 4, how many three-letter words related to coffee are there?

A. One   **C.** Two
B. None   **D.** Three

0672. Using Fig. 4, how many four-letter words related to coffee are there?

A. One   **C.** None
B. Three   **D.** Two

0673. Using Fig. 4, how many five-letter words related to coffee are there?

A. None   **C.** Three
B. One   **D.** Two

0674. Using Fig. 4, how many six-letter words related to coffee are there?

A. Two   **C.** Three
B. One   **D.** Four

0675. Using Fig. 4, how many seven-letter words related to coffee are there?

A. None   **C.** One
B. Two   **D.** Three

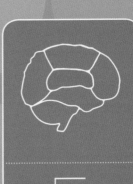

0676. Which letter is missing from the scrambled word below?

EIRLNPA

A. Y **C.** D
B. T **D.** A

0677. What is the meaning of the word "conspicuous"?

A. Noticeable **C.** Vague
B. Invisible **D.** Clear

0678. What is the meaning of the word "verisimilitude"?

A. A lie **C.** Adversity
B. Versatileness **D.** Resembles truth

0679. Under which category does the scrambled word below fall?

AOKORNAG

A. Fruit **C.** Vegetable
B. Animal **D.** City

0680. What does the puzzle below represent?

WHAT'S
TELEVISION

A. Television wattage
B. What is that sitting on the television?
C. What's on television?
D. Get off the television

0681. What does the phrase "A still tongue keeps a wise head" mean?

A. Intelligence is expressed in how well a person speaks
B. If you're quiet, people will know you're smart
C. Wise people don't talk much
D. If you talk about your problems, you'll feel better

0682. Solve the cryptogram below by deciphering the phrase, substituting numbers for letters. Under what category does the answer fit?

A	B	C	D	E	F	G	H	I	J	K	L	M

N	O	P	Q	R	S	T	U	V	W	X	Y	Z
12						7						

 7 15 15 21 9   15 21 12 26 12 18 7 5 14

- **A.** Song
- **B.** Place
- **C.** Movie
- **D.** Phrase

0683. I am the fifth letter in vacu_m and the fourth letter in min_scule. What letter am I? Hint: These words are so ostensible.

- **A.** M
- **B.** I
- **C.** U
- **D.** E

0684. Select the best word to complete the sentence below.

She listened to the _____ presentation.

- **A.** Oral
- **B.** Aural

0685. What does the term "déjà vu" mean?

- **A.** An embarrassing mistake
- **B.** Whatever one wants
- **C.** State of affairs
- **D.** Sense of having done something before

0686. What is the meaning of the word "raconteur"?

- **A.** A professional carpenter
- **B.** A skilled storyteller
- **C.** An adept teacher
- **D.** A thief

MOTIVATION IS KEY

Motivation is a key element in improving brain span. PBS documented motivation as one of seven principles necessary to improve your brain's capabilities. What does this mean to you? In other words, you must truly want a more efficient brain. It isn't enough to know your brain is short-circuiting and to put minimal effort into cognitive exercise. You must act on your desire to "grow" your brain. Like anything in life, effort is rewarded. Improving your brain span is not always easy, which you'll note as you tackle some of the more difficult tasks in this book. However, you will see the fruits of your labor as you begin to answer questions easily and process information quickly; you'll be well on your way to a sharper mind!

0687. What is the meaning of the phrase, "A bird in the hand is worth two in the bush"?

    A. Having one caged bird is better than two free birds
    B. Having something now is better than waiting for it
    C. Having something definite is better than something that is uncertain, even if it seems more promising
    D. Having something now is the same as having something better in the future

0688. What is the meaning of the phrase, "A rolling stone gathers no moss"?

    A. It's better to be unencumbered
    B. People who keep moving stay clean
    C. If you keep moving, you will not establish relationships
    D. Moving stones are cleaner than stationary ones

0689. What is the meaning of the phrase, "The calm before the storm"?

    A. The eye of the hurricane
    B. The wind is very still until thunder and lightning start
    C. People are quiet until the weather is bad
    D. The tranquil time prior to a rough period

0690. What is the meaning of the phrase, "As you sow, so shall you reap"?

    A. If you plant one crop, you will grow the same crop
    B. You will be rewarded for good deeds
    C. Your actions will determine your outcomes
    D. Bad deeds will be punished

0691. Which of the following proverbs is most similar to saying "All that glitters is not gold"?

    A. "A penny found is a penny earned"
    B. "The grass is always greener on the other side"
    C. "Beauty is in the eye of the beholder"
    D. "Don't judge a book by its cover"

0692. Which letter is missing from the scrambled word below?

HIBAN

A. G   **C.** T
B. P   **D.** S

0693. Which letter is missing from the scrambled word below?

LGNAEGA

A. U   **C.** S
B. N   **D.** T

0694. What is a seven-letter medical term for the wasting away of muscle tissue?

A. Rupture   **C.** Shrinks
B. Swelled   **D.** Atrophy

0695. Select the best word to complete the sentence below.

He _____ to her demands.

A. Exceeded
B. Acceded

0696. Select the best word to complete the sentence below.

He _____ his rights to a speedy trial.

A. Waved
B. Waived

0697. What is the meaning of the word "bumptious"?

A. Friendly   **C.** Humble
B. Nice   **D.** Aggressive

0698. Solve the cryptogram below by deciphering the phrase, substituting numbers for letters. Under what category does the answer fit?

A	B	C	D	E	F	G	H	I	J	K	L	M
											21	

N	O	P	Q	R	S	T	U	V	W	X	Y	Z
					9							

9 14 21 4 18 12 4   16 7

15 22 4   21 3 13 20 9

A. Phrase   **C.** Song
B. Game   **D.** Movie

0699. You have two minutes to use the letters below to create words, using each letter only once. Press the ⏱ on the Coach, then complete the task as quickly as you can. How many words did you create?

A. More than 25   **C.** 15–20
B. 20–25   **D.** Less than 15

0700. What does the puzzle below represent?

	YEAR
SCORE	YEAR
SCORE	YEAR
SCORE	YEAR
SCORE	YEAR
	YEAR
	YEAR

A. Seven years after the score
B. Keep a tally of the years
C. Scores of time
D. Four score and seven years

0701. I am the seventh letter of accept_ble and the tenth letter in indispens_ble. What letter am I? Hint: I'm sure this seems intangible.

    A. A   **C.** E

    B. I   **D.** U

0702. Which word is spelled incorrectly in the sentence below?

Misspelled words are printed in brochures and pamphlets occassionally.

    A. Misspelled   **C.** Occassionally

    B. Brochures   **D.** Pamphlets

0703. Which word is used incorrectly in the sentence below?

We knew their would be heck to pay for his egregious behavior.

    A. Knew   **C.** Their

    B. Egregious   **D.** Behavior

0704. Which word is used incorrectly in the sentence below?

Insurance companies except voluminous extracted data from public sources.

    A. Except   **C.** Extracted

    B. Voluminous **D.** Sources

0705. What does the puzzle below represent?

M
O
U
← 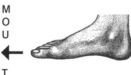
T
H

    A. Putting your foot in your mouth

    B. Hoof-and-mouth disease

    C. Kicked in the mouth

    D. Open mouth, insert foot

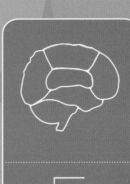

0706. Solve the cryptogram below by deciphering the phrase, substituting numbers for letters. Under what category does the answer fit?

A	B	C	D	E	F	G	H	I	J	K	L	M
				5								

N	O	P	Q	R	S	T	U	V	W	X	Y	Z

$$\overline{14}\ \overline{5}\ \overline{5}\ \overline{12}\ \overline{21}\ \overline{7}\ \overline{5}$$

   A. Song   **C.** Game
   B. Movie   **D.** Hairstyle

0707. Which word is spelled incorrectly in the sentence below?

A guilty conscience proves embarassing when we accidentally misspeak the truth.

   A. Conscience   **C.** Accidentally
   B. Embarassing   **D.** Misspeak

0708. Which word has an alternate spelling in the sentence below?

We recommend using good judgement when adapting the rhythm or cadence of renowned poetry.

   A. Recommend   **C.** Rhythm
   B. Judgement   **D.** Renowned

0709. Which word is spelled incorrectly in the sentence below?

Government requires our gubernatorial leaders to defend the bureacracies they represent for financial viability.

   A. Government   **C.** Gubernatorial
   B. Bureacracies   **D.** Viability

0710. What is the meaning of the word "pugnacious"?

   A. Quarrelsome   **C.** Doggish
   B. Beneficent   **D.** Pungent

FLEX YOUR MIND

Today's science assures us that our brain is pliable. This means that exercising your brain can help you maintain and improve your cognition. There is growing evidence that supports the need to treat your brain like any other muscle in your body. Take this information, and use it to work out your brain much like you would work out your heart and lungs. Exercises like the ones in this book are incredibly beneficial. There are other exercises you can do as well— crossword puzzles, word searches, Sudoku, etc. These exercises are also helpful if they truly challenge your mind.

0711. Which letters complete the word in the following sentence?

A teeny tiny piece, barely visible is _ _ _ u _ _ u _ e.

A. MIN; SC; L C. MIN; SK; L
B. MIN; AT; R D. MIN; TI; A

0712. Which of the following words is spelled correctly?

A. Irresistible C. Iresistable
B. Iresistible D. Irresistabel

0713. Which of the following words is spelled correctly?

A. Necessary C. Necesary
B. Neccessary D. Necissary

0714. Which of the following words is spelled correctly?

A. Conscous C. Consious
B. Conscious D. Concious

0715. What words are missing from the saying below?

Where sense is _____, everything is _____.

A. Wanting, Wanting
B. Present, Present
C. Lacking, Lacking
D. Known, Known

0716. What word is missing from the saying below?

Common sense is not so _____.

A. Useful C. Good
B. Sensational D. Common

0717. What word is missing from the saying below?

Beauty provoketh _____ sooner than gold.

A. Thieves C. Enemies
B. Friends D. Love

0718. What word is missing from the saying below?

An undutiful daughter will prove an _____ wife.

    A. Undisciplined
    B. Obligatory
    C. Unmanageable
    D. Irresponsible

0719. What word is missing from the saying below?

Forgive your _____ but never forget their names.

    A. Friends   **C.** Family
    B. Enemies   **D.** Name

0720. What words are missing from the saying below?

When one door closes another door _____; but we so often look so long and so regretfully upon the closed door, that we do not see the ones which _____ for us.

    A. Closes, Close
    B. Opens, Open
    C. Appears, Appear
    D. Swings shut, Shut

0721. What word is missing from the saying below?

Courage is knowing what not to _____.

    A. Do   **C.** Have
    B. Fear   **D.** See

0722. What words are missing from the saying below?

Be civil to _____; sociable to _____; familiar to _____.

    A. Few, Many, All   **C.** Many, Few, All
    B. All, Few, Man   **D.** All, Many, Few

0723. What word is missing from the saying below?

A true _____ is one soul in two bodies.

    A. Enemy   **C.** Friend
    B. Lover   **D.** Sister

0724. What word is missing from the saying below?

A great city is not to be confounded with a(n) _____ one.

A. Small   **C.** Populous
B. Large   **D.** Unpopulated

0725. What word is missing from the saying below?

Old _____ never die, they simply fade away.

A. Friends   **C.** Soldiers
B. Stars   **D.** Acquaintances

0726. What words are missing from the saying below?

Old habits _____ _____.

A. Die hard   **C.** Die fast
B. Never die   **D.** Live on

0727. What words are missing from the saying below?

No news is _____ _____.

A. Bad news   **C.** Good news
B. Some news   **D.** No news

0728. What word is missing from the saying below?

_____ makes the heart grow fonder.

A. Absence   **C.** Wisdom
B. Love   **D.** Friendship

0729. What is the meaning of the word "cathartic"?

A. Emotional satisfaction
B. Emotional release
C. Physical satisfaction
D. To scream

0730. What words are missing from the saying below?

Beauty is only _____ _____.

    A. Skin deep   **C.** Fair
    B. For a while   **D.** For women

0731. What word is missing from the saying below?

Better late than _____.

    A. Early   **C.** Yesterday
    B. Tomorrow   **D.** Never

0732. What word is missing from the saying below?

Nothing ventured, nothing _____.

    A. Lost   **C.** Gained
    B. Found   **D.** Sent

0733. What words are missing from the saying below?

One man's _____ is another man's_____.

    A. Gain, Loss   **C.** Love, Hate
    B. Loss, Gain   **D.** Hobby, Boredom

0734. What word is missing from the saying below?

_____ is next to Godliness.

    A. Kindness   **C.** Holiness
    B. Goodness   **D.** Cleanliness

0735. What words are missing from the saying below?

The first step is always _____ _____.

    A. The easiest   **C.** The fastest
    B. The hardest   **D.** The slowest

LANGUAGE

0724–
0735

READING COMPREHENSION

We all have difficulty comprehending what we are reading sometimes. This is particularly true if the material is difficult or we are not interested in it. If you are attempting to digest challenging material, it's best to do it when you are alert (e.g., not before bed!). Eliminate distractions, and take frequent breaks. It's also helpful to highlight important sentences and jot notes in the sidelines to refresh your memory. That also helps to ensure you are getting the primary points. If your mind is wandering, take a break, or let your mind fully engage in the intruding thought—putting an interrupting thought in abeyance frequently serves as a further distraction until it finally forces you to give it top priority. Try this as you work through this book: If you are working on a particularly difficult question, give it your full attention. If you are not able to, skip to the next question—the Coach will bring you back to that question at another time.

FIGURE 5

The inquisitive young lady queried the staunch gentleman who quietly requested she contain her curiousity.

0736. Read Fig. 5. Which two words are synonyms?

    A. Inquisitive, Curiousity
    B. Young, Staunch
    C. Queried, Requested
    D. Quietly, Contained

0737. Read Fig. 5. Which word is misspelled?

    A. Inquisitive   **C.** Staunch
    B. Queried   **D.** Curiousity

0738. Read Fig. 5. What part of speech is "curiosity"?

    A. Adjective   **C.** Adverb
    B. Verb   **D.** Noun

0739. Read Fig. 5. What is the section " . . . who quietly requested . . ." called?

    A. Predicate
    B. Prepositional phrase
    C. Past participle
    D. Conjunction

0740. Read Fig. 5. "Inquisitive" is what part of speech in this sentence?

    A. Adjective
    B. Adverb
    C. Noun
    D. Interjection

LANGUAGE

0736–0740

FIGURE 6

Holy mackerel, it is much later than I thought!

0741. Read Fig. 6. "Holy mackerel" is which part of speech?

    A. Conjunction   **C.** Interrogative
    B. Interjection   **D.** Adjective

0742. Read Fig. 6. What type of sentence is this?

    A. Interrogative   **C.** Explanatory
    B. Exclamatory   **D.** Narrative

0743. Read the sentence below. What type of sentence is this?

What time is it?

    A. Exclamation   **C.** Interrogative
    B. Modifier   **D.** Interjection

0744. Read the sentence below. Which word is misspelled?

The adventurous Olympian enjoyed the vigorous and gruling schedule associated with mountain climbing.

    A. Adventurous   **C.** Gruling
    B. Olympian   **D.** Associated

0745. You have two minutes to use the letters below to create words, using each letter only once. Press the ⏱ on the Coach, then complete the task as quickly as you can. How many words did you create?

JaiNdeLdfaNDfWmRkSdfSEFpaDEvAMzQoUc

    A. More than 20   **C.** 14–17
    B. 17–20   **D.** Less than 14

0746. What does the word "rendezvous" mean?

    A. An affair
    B. My fault
    C. A meeting place
    D. Specifically unwelcome

0747. What does the term "tête-à-tête" mean?

    A. Enjoyment
    B. Reason for being
    C. Spirit of times
    D. Head-to-head

0748. What is an antonym for "grueling"?

    A. Cakewalk   **C.** Tough
    B. Vigorous   **D.** Exhausting

0749. What is an alternate meaning for "gruel"?

    A. Duel   **C.** Exhume
    B. Unkind   **D.** Cereal-like substance

0750. Solve the cryptogram below by deciphering the phrase, substituting numbers for letters. Under what category does the answer fit?

A	B	C	D	E	F	G	H	I	J	K	L	M
				5				9				

N	O	P	Q	R	S	T	U	V	W	X	Y	Z
12												

13 9 4 12 9 17 11 20   9 12   20 11 5

17 6 26 4 5 12   7 13   17 7 7 4

6 12 4   5 14 9 22

    A. Song   **C.** Game
    B. Novel   **D.** Hairstyle

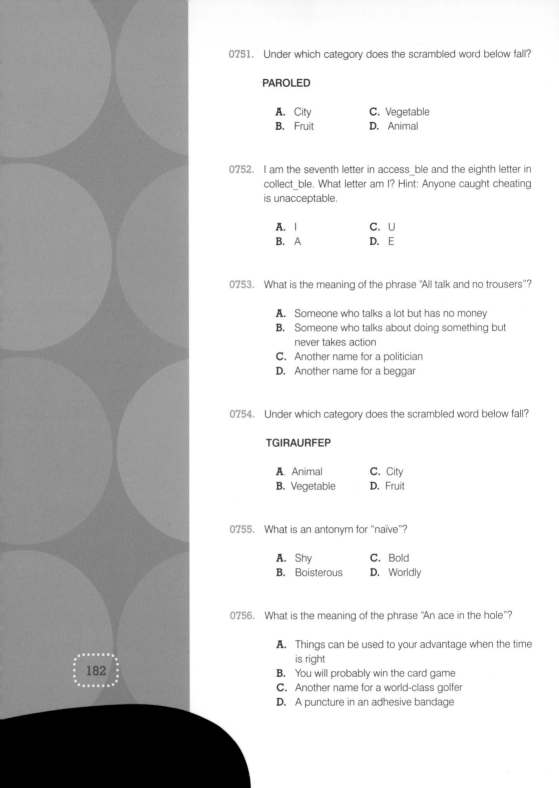

0751. Under which category does the scrambled word below fall?

PAROLED

    A. City   **C.** Vegetable
    B. Fruit   **D.** Animal

0752. I am the seventh letter in access_ble and the eighth letter in collect_ble. What letter am I? Hint: Anyone caught cheating is unacceptable.

    A. I   **C.** U
    B. A   **D.** E

0753. What is the meaning of the phrase "All talk and no trousers"?

    A. Someone who talks a lot but has no money
    B. Someone who talks about doing something but never takes action
    C. Another name for a politician
    D. Another name for a beggar

0754. Under which category does the scrambled word below fall?

TGIRAURFEP

    A. Animal   **C.** City
    B. Vegetable   **D.** Fruit

0755. What is an antonym for "naïve"?

    A. Shy   **C.** Bold
    B. Boisterous   **D.** Worldly

0756. What is the meaning of the phrase "An ace in the hole"?

    A. Things can be used to your advantage when the time is right
    B. You will probably win the card game
    C. Another name for a world-class golfer
    D. A puncture in an adhesive bandage

0757. Solve the cryptogram below by deciphering the phrase, substituting numbers for letters. Under what category does the answer fit?

A	B	C	D	E	F	G	H	I	J	K	L	M
								19				

N	O	P	Q	R	S	T	U	V	W	X	Y	Z
8												

$\overline{19}\ \overline{3}\ \overline{14}\ \overline{7}\quad \overline{20}\ \overline{8}\ \overline{11}\quad \overline{19}\ \overline{8}\ \overline{5}$

A. Phrase   C. Movie
B. Song   D. Novel

0758. What is a synonym for "forthright"?

A. Truthful   C. Direct
B. Denies   D. Unaware

0759. What is an antonym for "tranquil"?

A. Chaotic   C. Rough
B. Peaceful   D. Talkative

0760 What is a homonym for "aisle"?

A. Mile   C. Ale
B. Isle   D. Row

0761. What is a homonym for "him"?

A. Hymn   C. Swim
B. He   D. She

0762. Select the best word to complete the sentence below.

The _____ clashed loudly.

A. Symbols   **C.** Simbols
B. Cimbals   **D.** Cymbals

0763. Select the best word to complete the sentence below.

Her _____ fills the room with a special warmth.

A. Presents   **C.** Presence
B. Appearance   **D.** Presensce

0764. Select the best word to complete the sentence below.

I heard the boy _____ when the teacher assigned homework.

A. Grown   **C.** Grow
B. Grone   **D.** Groan

0765. Select the best word to complete the sentence below.

Is that boat for _____?

A. Sale   **C.** Sell
B. Sail   **D.** Sold

0766. What is the meaning of the word "diction"?

A. Tone   **C.** Catchphrase
B. Word choice   **D.** Shorthand

0767. What is the picture of below?

A. Jester   **C.** Elf
B. Joker   **D.** Clown

0768. Which of the following is an acronym?

    A. UFO   **C.** Paris
    B. Weds.   **D.** Their

0769. "Malayalam" is an example of which type of word?

    A. Anagram
    B. Acronym
    C. Palindrome
    D. Homonym

0770. What does the acronym "AP" stand for?

    A. April
    B. American Psychiatric Association
    C. All People
    D. Associated Press

0771. What is a palindrome for a "lady"?

    A. Miss   **C.** Ms.
    B. Madam **D.** Mrs.

0772. What is the picture of below?

    A. Lacrosse stick
    B. Hockey stick
    C. Polo stick
    D. Racquetball racket

0773. What is the picture of below?

    A. Compact   **C.** Tweezers
    B. Compass   **D.** Knife

0774. What is the meaning of the word "caveat"?

    A. Warning
    B. Unconditional love
    C. A slow-moving animal
    D. Interest

0775. What is the meaning of the phrase, "A watched pot never boils"?

    A. If you walk away from the stove, the food will cook
    B. Some things work out in their own time. So if you are impatient, it will only make things seem to take longer to be resolved or fixed
    C. The pasta will never get done if you keep stirring it
    D. If you are always watching someone, then they'll do what's right

0776. What does the puzzle shown at right represent?

    A. A stitch in time
    B. Sitting backwards before me
    C. It is inside of time
    D. Is it home?

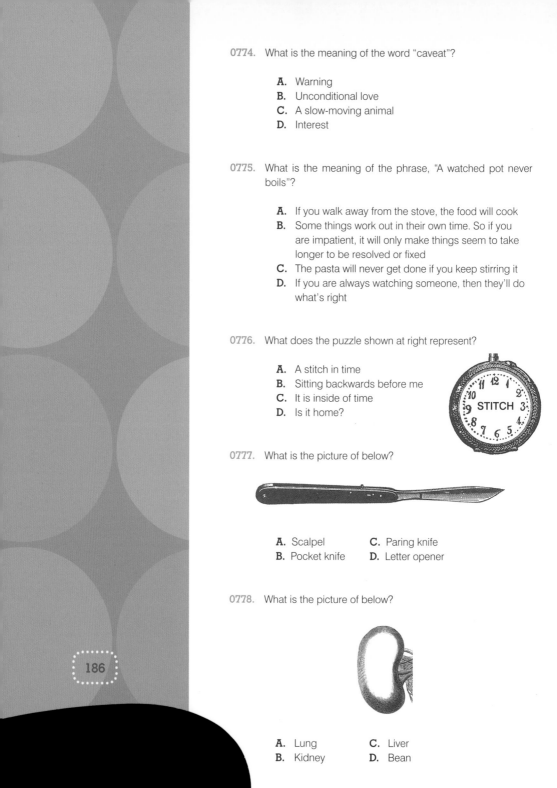

0777. What is the picture of below?

    A. Scalpel   **C.** Paring knife
    B. Pocket knife   **D.** Letter opener

0778. What is the picture of below?

    A. Lung   **C.** Liver
    B. Kidney   **D.** Bean

0779. What is the picture of below?

A. Cocoon	**C.** Web
B. Egg	**D.** Caterpillar

0780. What is the picture of below?

A. Feather	**C.** Quill
B. Vein	**D.** Spine

0781. What is the picture of below?

A. Tumble weed	**C.** Sea urchin
B. Pom-pom	**D.** Coral

0782. What is the picture of below?

A. Girdle	**C.** Camisole
B. Corset	**D.** Vest

0783.   What is the picture of below?

A. Croquet mallet	**C.** Pounder
B. Hammer	**D.** Hatchet

0784.   What is the picture of below?

A. Scissors	**C.** Clasp
B. Tongs	**D.** Tweezers

0785.   What is the picture of below?

A. Pirouette	**C.** Dress stand
B. Umbrella	**D.** Parasol

0786.   What is the picture of below?

A. Bar	**C.** Pipes
B. Tube	**D.** Wicket

0787. What is the picture of below?

    A. Manikin   **C.** Prosthesis
    B. Cast   **D.** Amputation

0788. Big is to Small as Short is _____?

    A. Small   **C.** Big
    B. Long   **D.** Tall

0789. Eye is to Hurricane as N is to _____?

    A. Alphabet   **C.** Letters
    B. Attention   **D.** Spelling

0790. Salt is to Ham as _____ is to Cosmetics?

    A. Formaldehyde   **C.** Powder
    B. Color   **D.** Brush

0791. Director is to Band as Metal is to _____?

    A. Electricity   **C.** Screw
    B. Sheet   **D.** Shed

0792. Eat is to Ate as Go is to _____?

    A. Gone   **C.** Do
    B. Going   **D.** Back

0793. Fire is to Fireplace as Car is to _____?

    A. House   **C.** Drive
    B. Garage   **D.** Parking spot

0794. Pages are to Book as Seconds are to_____?

    A. Time   **C.** Minute
    B. Milliseconds   **D.** Library

DEPRESSION

Depression, of the mental health variety, can become prevalent with aging and life changes. It can have a profound impact on cognitive abilities, including memory, manifesting particularly in forgetfulness. In fact, sometimes depression can impair your ability to remember to the extent that it creates pseudodementia (or false dementia). Pseudo-dementia usually involves memory loss, but it is memory loss due to inattention, rather than an inability to encode new information as found in dementia. Depression is a common illness and can be very treatable. If you think you might be depressed, you should consult your physician.

0795. Bunny is to Rabbit as Fawn is to _____?

    A. Cow   **C.** Horse
    B. Lamb   **D.** Deer

0796. Vein is to Blood as Hose is to _____?

    A. Yard   **C.** Air
    B. Water   **D.** Soil

0797. 26 is to alphabet as 42.2 is to _____?

    A. Gold   **C.** 6 weeks
    B. Quart   **D.** Marathon

0798. Left is to Logic as Right is to _____?

    A. Creativity   **C.** Language
    B. Turn   **D.** Correct

0799. Paddle is to Canoe as Reins are to _____?

    A. Steer   **C.** Gear
    B. Saddle   **D.** Horse

0800. Fork is to Utensil as Hammer is to _____?

    A. Nail   **C.** Tool
    B. Toolbox   **D.** Mallet

VISUAL PROCESSING

FORM & SPATIAL PROCESSING

O ver 30 percent of the brain's mass and function is devoted to some form of visual processing. The visual systems within the brain utilize a vast amount of the overall energy of the users. As a matter of fact, the visual systems are so complex that it is estimated they use over 30 percent of the body's caloric consumption just when the body is at rest.

The brain has multiple visual systems, and eyes are just a minute part. The eyes are actually simple sensors and do not allow us to see whatsoever. The eyes only serve to send fairly simple signals to the back region of the brain, where the information is processed and integrated into vision. It is the brain that sees. It is the mind that perceives.

Two of the primary visual systems are the Ventral Visual Stream (or "circuit") and the Dorsal Visual Stream. The Ventral Visual Stream serves to answer the question of what something is. This is also referred to as Form vision. The Dorsal Visual Stream answers the question of where something is, also called Spatial Processing. There are also individual systems dedicated to such complex functions as recognizing faces, perceiving motion, color differentiation, part-to-whole integration, pattern recognition, and the list goes on. Vision is so important that we have a whole lobe devoted to its function. This occipital lobe is in the back of the brain and is connected to vast networks throughout the mind.

Because of the power and energy inherent to the visual system, it serves as an excellent modality to improve other brain functions. Focus, attention, memory, and even language can all be greatly enhanced if processed through vision. For example, associate a visual cue when trying to remember someone's name. Or picture yourself succeeding in any given situation. Can't remember a word? Try to see it. Need to remember to pick up groceries? Take a moment and, in your "mind's eye," picture a gallon of milk chasing a loaf of bread down the cold aisle of the grocery store as it throws eggs. We are visual creatures, and vision is the foundation of improving cognition.

Within this chapter, the Coach will lead you through a variety of visual challenges. You will be presented with complex visual fields and be challenged to find subtle similarities and differences. You will identify and complete patterns and solve abstract visual puzzles. The level of detail you will begin to notice will amaze you!

FIGURE 1

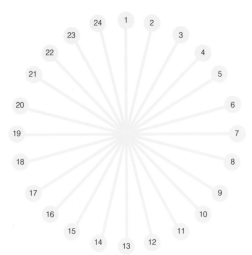

0801. Using Fig. 1, which angle numbers match the angles of the lines shown at right?

   A. 13, 10   **C.** 14, 12
   B. 13, 11   **D.** 13, 9

0802. Using Fig. 1, which angle numbers match the angles of the lines shown at right?

   A. 16, 5   **C.** 16, 6
   B. 17, 5   **D.** 17, 6

0803. Using Fig. 1, which angle numbers match the angles of the lines shown at right?

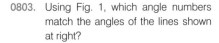

   A. 21, 18   **C.** 21, 19
   B. 22, 17   **D.** 22, 16

0804. Using Fig. 1, which angle numbers match the angles of the lines shown at right?

   A. 5, 15   **C.** 5, 16
   B. 4, 15   **D.** 4, 14

0805. Using Fig. 1, which angle numbers match the angles of the lines shown at right?

A. 24, 3 **C.** 22, 3
B. 23, 3 **D.** 23, 4

0806. Using Fig. 1, which angle numbers match the angles of the lines shown at right?

A. 2, 9 **C.** 2, 10
B. 2, 8 **D.** 1, 9

FIGURE 2

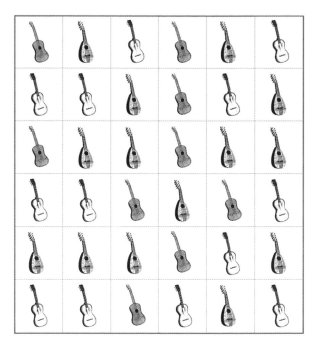

0807. How many times is the sequence of three items shown at right repeated in Fig. 2? The sequence can be found horizontally, vertically, and reversed.

A. Four **C.** Two
B. Three **D.** Five

FIGURE 3

USE COMMON SENSES

Our five senses—sight, smell, hearing, touch, and taste—are our links to the outside world. They are the means by which we experience everything around us. The senses are therefore, a natural way to enhance cognition and memory. If you want to remember something, think about how it tastes, smells, feels, looks, or sounds. The more ridiculous the better, such as the sight and sound of cotton balls bouncing around your bathroom, if you need to be certain to buy cotton balls at the store.

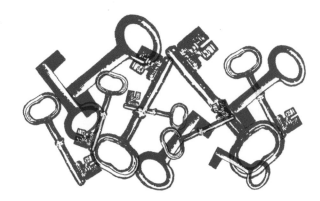

0808. Review Fig. 3. How many keys are there?

    A. Seven   **C.** Five
    B. Six   **D.** Eight

0809. Review Fig. 3. How many keys are there?

    A. Four   **C.** Five
    B. Six   **D.** Seven

0810. What would the item be if you assembled the pieces shown at right?

    A. Pocket watch
    B. Building
    C. Broom
    D. Vest

0811. What would the item be if you assembled the pieces shown at right?

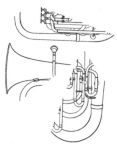

    A. Trumpet
    B. French horn
    C. Saxophone
    D. Tuba

0812. What time does the clock shown below reflect?

    A. 2:38:15   **C.** 2:39
    B. 2:38:16   **D.** 3:54

0813. What is missing from the clock shown at right?

    A. Second hand
    B. I in Roman numeral 8
    C. Tick mark at 54 seconds
    D. Clasp

0814. Using the clock shown above, which of the following Roman numerals is written incorrectly?

    A. VIII   **C.** IX
    B. IIII   **D.** XI

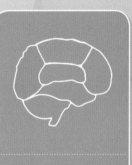

0815. You have fifteen seconds to study the picture shown at right. Press the ↻ on the Coach, then answer the question as quickly as you can. [STOP] What is missing from the picture?

    A. One handlebar
    B. Pedal
    C. Seat
    D. Chain

0816. You have fifteen seconds to study the picture below. Press the ↻ on the Coach, then answer the question as quickly as you can. [STOP] What is missing from the picture?

    A. Rearview Mirror
    B. Headlight
    C. Bumper
    D. Part of grill

0817. Who is this famous person shown at right?

    A. John F. Kennedy
    B. Richard Nixon
    C. Robert F. Kennedy
    D. George Wallace

FIGURE 4

0818. Which leaf from Fig. 4 matches the leaf shown at right?

   A. J   **C.** H
   B. L   **D.** A

0819. The leaf shown at right is in the center of which two leaves in Fig. 4?

   A. B and C   **C.** J and K
   B. E and F   **D.** None of these

0820. Which of the following leaves from Fig. 4 is *not* next to the leaf shown at right?

   A. F   **C.** D
   B. C   **D.** G

0821. Which leaf from Fig. 4 matches the leaf shown at right?

   A. D   **C.** C
   B. I   **D.** E

0822. The tip of the leaf shown at right points in which direction in Fig. 4?

    A. Right   **C.** Left
    B. Down   **D.** Up

0823. The leaf shown at right touches which leaves in Fig. 4?

    A. A, D, H   **C.** B, K
    B. A, E, F   **D.** E, F

0824. Which of the following pieces correctly completes the picture shown at right?

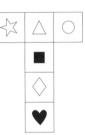

    A.   C.

    B.   D.

0825. Which of the following cubes is the same as the unfolded cube shown at right?

    A.   C.

    B.   D.

0826. Which of the following images best depicts a tree during the spring season?

    A.   C.

    B.   D.

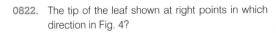

0827. Who is this famous person shown at right?

    A. Madame Curie
    B. Joan of Arc
    C. Mother Theresa
    D. Catherine the Great

0828. You have fifteen seconds to study the two pictures below. Press the ◐ on the Coach, then answer the question as quickly as you can.

How are they different?

    A. Last staff is shorter
    B. Tip of third crown is missing
    C. Ponytails are different lengths
    D. One foot is missing

0829. You have fifteen seconds to study the two pictures below. Press the ◐ on the Coach, then answer the question as quickly as you can.

How are they different?

    A. Lady's hand is missing
    B. One flower is missing
    C. Gentleman's foot is missing
    D. Lady's bow is missing

0830. You have fifteen seconds to study the picture below. Press the ◔ on the Coach, then answer the question as quickly as you can.

What is missing from the picture?

A. Propeller **C.** Part of skid
B. Tail rotor **D.** Part of main rotor

0831. You have fifteen seconds to study the picture below. Press the ◔ on the Coach, then answer the question as quickly as you can.

What is missing from the picture?

A. Mother's foot **C.** Bottom of hair
B. Leg of table **D.** Mother's hand

0832. You have fifteen seconds to study the two pictures below. Press the ◔ on the Coach, then answer the question as quickly as you can.

How are they different?

A. Fruit on bottom right is darkened
B. Leaf on bottom right is missing
C. Root is missing
D. One less horizontal line

VISUAL TIPS

When studying the pictures in this category, begin by looking at edges and main portions of each image before honing in on the minute details. For instance, for Figures 4 and 6 on pages 198 and 204, look at the tips of the leaves before looking at the interior veins. For assembly questions, like those on this page, look at the surroundings. Sometimes this will help identify the actual object. And for all questions, when all else fails, use the process of elimination. Rule out the choices you know are incorrect, and then study the remaining selections.

0833. What would the item be if you assembled the pieces shown at right?

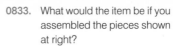

A. Spinning wheel
B. Wind mill
C. Lamp without shade
D. Propeller

0834. What would the item be if you assembled the pieces shown at right?

A. Heart
B. Bird
C. Fan
D. Shell

0835. What would the item be if you assembled the pieces shown at right?

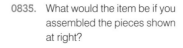

A. Heart
B. Butterfly
C. Veins
D. Ribs

0836. What would the item be if you assembled the pieces shown at right?

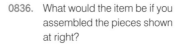

A. Clock
B. Bicycle tire
C. Orange slice
D. Harp

0837. What would the item be if you assembled the pieces shown at right?

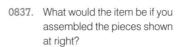

A. Cup
B. Bell
C. Urn
D. Anvil

0838. What would the item be if you assemble the pieces shown at right?

    A. Brush
    B. Crown
    C. Skillet
    D. Trivet

0839. What would the item be if you assembled the pieces shown at right?

    A. Compass
    B. Phonograph
    C. Desk clock
    D. Weather station

0840. If you were to assemble the pieces shown at right, one of the pieces would *not* fit. Which one?

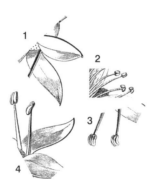

    A. Piece 5
    B. Piece 2
    C. Piece 3
    D. Piece 1

FIGURE 5

0841. How many times is the pattern shown at right repeated in Fig. 5? Hint: The pattern may be turned in different directions.

    A. Five   **C.** Two
    B. Four   **D.** Three

FIGURE 6

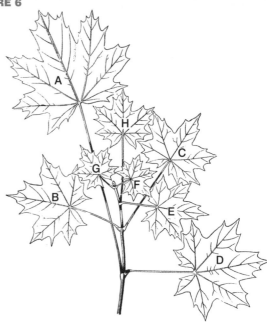

0842. Which leaf from Fig. 6 is the other half of the leaf shown at right?

    A. C   **C.** B
    B. D   **D.** E

0843. The leaf portion shown at right belongs to which leaf in Fig. 6?

    A. D   **C.** B
    B. A   **D.** C

0844. The leaf tip shown at right is adjacent to which leaf in Fig. 6?

    A. E   **C.** F
    B. C   **D.** D

0845. Which leaf in Fig. 6 is the other half of the leaf shown at right?

    A. B   **C.** H
    B. G   **D.** E

0846. Which leaves in Fig. 6 match the leaves shown at right?

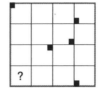

- **A.** E and F
- **C.** H and C
- **B.** B and G
- **D.** D and E

0847. Study the diagram shown at right. Which of the following squares would complete the sequence?

- **A.**
- **C.**
- **B.**
- **D.**

0848. You have fifteen seconds to study the design below. Press the ↻ on the Coach, then answer the question as quickly as you can.

Which of the following pieces completes the picture?

- **A.**
- **C.**
- **B.**
- **D.**

0849. Who is this famous person shown at right?

- **A.** Jimmy Carter
- **B.** Bill Clinton
- **C.** Richard Nixon
- **D.** Walter Cronkite

0850. How many four-sided figures are included in the picture shown at right?

- **A.** Twelve
- **C.** Sixteen
- **B.** Eleven
- **D.** Eighteen

VITAMIN B$_{12}$

Vitamin B$_{12}$ plays an important role in maintaining healthy red blood cells and nerve cells. The body stores Vitamin B$_{12}$ very well, so it's unusual to have low levels of this vitamin. Those at risk for low B$_{12}$ levels can include the elderly, vegans, and Crohn's sufferers. Even slightly lowered levels of B$_{12}$ may result in unusual psychiatric and neurological symptoms, including depression, dementia, low blood pressure, and muscle weakness, among other symptoms. If you are experiencing any of these symptoms, it is important to have your levels of vitamin B$_{12}$ checked. It is also important to consult your physician before starting a regimen of B$_{12}$ as it is contraindicated in some disorders and overdosing can cause complications.

0851. What does the rebus shown at right represent?

    A. Sister   **C.** Brother
    B. Father   **D.** Mother

0852. What does the rebus shown at right represent?

    A. Bug in the hole   **C.** Pass the butter
    B. Hold the butter   **D.** Behold

0853. What does the rebus shown at right represent?

    A. Dessert
    B. Pancake
    C. Cupcake
    D. Happiness

0854. What does the rebus shown at right represent?

    A. As time goes by
    B. Time on my hands
    C. Rock around the clock
    D. Killing time

0855. How are the two images shown at right different?

    A. Toe is missing
    B. Pattern on head is different
    C. Shell pattern is different
    D. Tail length is different

0856. How is the image on the right different from the image on the left?

    A. They are the same
    B. Something is missing
    C. Something was added

0857. In what order should the pieces shown below be placed to complete the vertically oriented picture?

1   2   3   4

A. 2, 1, 4, 3   **C.** 2, 3, 1, 4
B. 2, 4, 1, 3   **D.** 2, 4, 3, 1

FIGURE 7

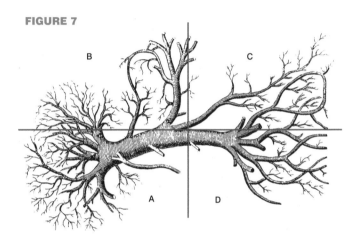

0858. From which section in Fig. 7 does the enlarged picture shown at right come?

A. Section D
B. Section A
C. Section C
D. Section B

0859. Study the picture shown below, then answer the question.

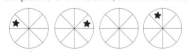

Which of the following diagrams would complete the sequence?

A.   **C.**

B.   **D.**

0860. In what order should the pieces shown below be placed to complete the vertically oriented picture?

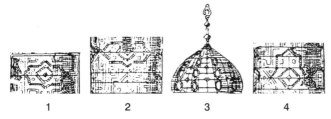

1   2   3   4

    A. 3, 1, 4, 2   **C.** 3, 1, 2, 4
    B. 3, 4, 2, 1   **D.** 3, 2, 4, 1

FIGURE 8

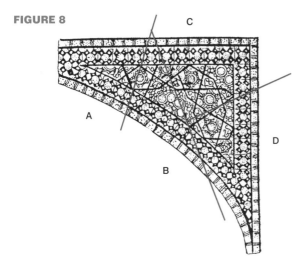

C

A

B

D

0861. From which section in Fig. 8 does the enlarged picture shown at right come?

    A. Section B   **C.** Section D
    B. Section A   **D.** Section C

0862. How many jigsaw pieces are shown at right?

    A. Seven
    B. Eight
    C. Ten
    D. Nine

0863. Study the diagram shown at right, then answer the question. Which of the following diagrams would complete the sequence?

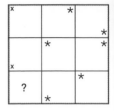

A. ☐ x

C. ☐ ★

B. x ☐

D. ☐ x

0864. How are the two images below different?

A. Part of ribbon missing
B. Tassel missing
C. Head of eagle darkened
D. Part of scrollwork missing on middle right

0865. How many lines are shown below?

A. Eighteen   C. Fifteen
B. Fourteen   D. Thirteen

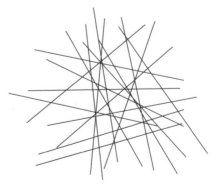

FIGURE 9

A ——————
B   ——————
C   ———————
D   ——————

0866. Study Fig. 9. Which line is longest?

    A. Line B   **C.** Line C
    B. Line A   **D.** Line D

0867. Study Fig. 9. Which line is shortest?

    A. Line A   **C.** Line C
    B. Line B   **D.** Line D

0868. Study the lines shown below. Which line is bisected exactly in half?

    A. Line D   **C.** Line A
    B. Line B   **D.** Line C

FIGURE 10

0869. From which section in Fig. 10 does the enlarged picture shown at right come?

    A. Section IV   **C.** Section II
    B. Section III   **D.** Section I

FIGURE 11

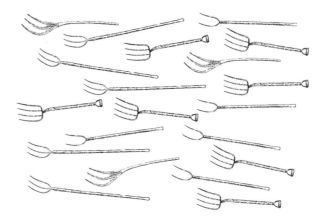

THAT'S FUNNY!

Humor is very important in helping to improve cognition. Humor distills stress—thus allowing your brain to relax and rid itself of negative energy. Humor can also be used to memorize. Think of a jug of milk running down the grocery aisle chasing a stick of butter as it throws eggs. Sound funny? Sure. But it may help you to remember to purchase milk, butter, and eggs at the grocery store.

0870. Which type of pitchfork is there the most of in Fig. 11?

    A. Four-prong pitchfork
    B. Narrow three-prong pitchfork
    C. Two-prong pitchfork
    D. Wide three-prong pitchfork

0871. Which type of pitchfork is there the least of in Fig. 11?

    A. Narrow three-prong pitchfork
    B. Two-prong pitchfork
    C. Wide three-prong pitchfork
    D. Four-prong pitchfork

0872. How many three-prong pitchforks are shown in Fig. 11?

    A. Eight   **C.** Six
    B. Five   **D.** Four

0873. You have fifteen seconds to study the picture shown at right. Press the ⟳ on the Coach, then answer the question as quickly as you can. [STOP] What is missing from the picture?

    A. White square in fourth column
    B. Black square in last column
    C. Black square in top row
    D. White square in third row

FIGURE 12

0874. How many times is the pattern shown at right repeated in Fig. 12? The pattern can be found horizontally, vertically, and reversed.

A. Four C. One
B. Two   D. Three

0875. What is the correct sequence of the pictures shown below?

I II III IV V

A. III, I, IV, II, V C. III, IV, I, II, V
B. I, IV, II, V, III   D. III, IV, I, V, II

FIGURE 13

0876. Which of the following pieces correctly completes Fig. 13?

 A.   B.   C.   D.

0877. Who is the famous person shown at right?

A. Sigmund Freud
B. Salvador Dalí
C. Albert Einstein
D. Peter Falk

0878. Which of the lines shown below is longest?

A   B   C   D

A. Line D   **C.** Line A
B. Line B   **D.** Line C

FIGURE 14

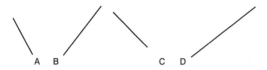

0879. Study Fig. 14. Which letter would come next in the sequence?

A. B. C. D.

FIGURE 15

A   B

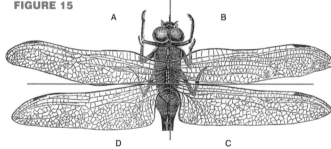

D   C

0880. From which section in Fig. 15 does the enlarged picture shown at right come?

A. Section D   **C.** Section C
B. Section B   **D.** Section A

0881. Review the grouped symbols shown below. Which symbol does *not* belong?

A   B   C   D

A. B   **C.** D
B. A   **D.** C

0882. You have fifteen seconds to study the two pictures shown below. Press the ⏱ on the Coach, then answer the question as quickly as you can.

How is the picture on the right different?

A. The dog's tail is missing
B. A coat button is missing from the third child's jacket
C. The girl's shoe buckle is missing
D. The boy on the left is missing his thumb

FIGURE 16

0883. How many times does the pattern shown at right repeat in Fig. 16? Pattern may be shown forward, backward, horizontally, or vertically.

A. Five   **C.** Four
B. Six   **D.** Three

0884. How many total tools are shown at right?

A. Nine   **C.** Eleven
B. Eight   **D.** Ten

0885. Which of the flowers shown below does *not* belong in the grouping?

1   2   3   4

A. Flower 3   **C.** Flower 2
B. Flower 1   **D.** Flower 4

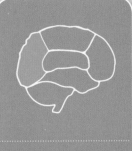

0886. Which insect shown below is different from all of the others in the grouping?

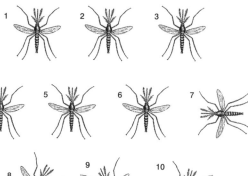

A. Insect 8   **C.** Insect 6
B. Insect 3   **D.** Insect 1

0887. Which two designs shown below are identical?

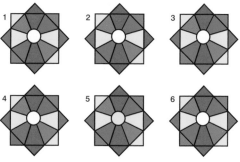

A. 1 and 4   **C.** 4 and 5
B. 2 and 3   **D.** 1 and 6

0888. Review the picture shown below. If the paper clip is 2 centimeters, approximately how long is the pencil?

A. 14 cm   **C.** 16 cm
B. 10 cm   **D.** 8 cm

FIGURE 17

0889. How many of the foods in Fig. 17 would you eat with syrup?

    A. One   **C.** Three
    B. Two   **D.** None

0890. Which item is pictured in Fig. 17 most frequently?

    A. Banana   **C.** Muffin
    B. Egg   **D.** Coffee with sugar

0891. How many items in Fig. 17 are *not* edible?

    A. None   **C.** Two
    B. One   **D.** Three

FIGURE 18

0892. Select the three butterflies shown below that comprise Fig. 18.

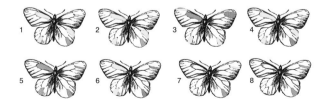

    A. 1, 2, 7   **C.** 2, 3, 7
    B. 2, 3, 8   **D.** 1, 2, 8

FIGURE 19

0893.   Which of the following shapes comprise Fig. 19?

A. 2, 4, 5   C. 2, 3, 4
B. 2, 5, 6   D. 2, 5, 8

FIGURE 20

	A	B	C	D	E
1	☆	○	□	☆	♡
2	♡	△	○	○	☆
3	□	☆	△	♡	○
4	☆	△	○	☆	♡
5	△	□	☆	△	○

0894.   Review Fig. 20. Which row or column contains five different shapes?

A. Column C   C. Row 5
B. Row 3   D. Column A

0895.   Review Fig. 20. Which row or column contains two hearts?

A. Column E   C. Row 1
B. Row 3   D. Column B

0896.   Review Fig. 20. How many rows and columns contain circles?

A. Seven   C. Ten
B. Eight   D. Nine

FIGURE 21

0897. Review Fig. 21. How many pennies are face-side-up?

    A. Eleven   **C.** Twelve
    B. Ten   **D.** Thirteen

0898. Review Fig. 21. How many coins are tail-side-up?

    A. Ten   **C.** Nine
    B. Eleven **D.** Seven

0899. Review Fig. 21. How many total coins are shown?

    A. Twenty-three   **C.** Twenty-eight
    B. Twenty-five   **D.** Twenty-four

0900. Review Fig. 21. Which of the following coins is *not* included?

    A. Quarters   **C.** Pennies
    B. Nickels   **D.** Dimes

0901. Look at the two snowflakes shown below. Which center
       diamond is larger?

    A. They are both the same
    B. The one on the left
    C. The one on the right

HYPNOSIS

Hypnosis is a powerful tool in learning to relax. We're not talking about the trancelike state you observe in demonstrations. Hypnosis in this sense is more of an exercise in meditation and guided imagery. You begin by making yourself physically comfortable. Frequently, hypnotherapists will guide you into a state of relaxation by tensing and releasing various muscle groups. You then allow your mind to drift off to an image of somewhere you feel free and calm—it may be a beach, the mountains, a cascading waterfall, or a beautiful garden. Add a touch of soft, gentle music, and you can begin to rid yourself of any unwanted negative energy that is clogging your brain.

FIGURE 22

0902. Apply the instructions below to Fig. 22 to visualize the shape.

Start at the second dot from the left in the bottom row, go up 2 dots, right 1 dot, up and right diagonally 1 dot, down 1 dot, left 1 dot, up 1 dot, left 2 dots, and down 2 dots.

Which of the following accurately reflects the shape?

A.   B.   C.   D.

0903. Apply the instructions below to Fig. 22 to visualize the shape.

Start in the bottom right corner, go up 2 dots, left 2 dots, down 2 dots, and right 2 dots.

What shape did you draw?

    A. Diamond   **C.** Square
    B. Rectangle   **D.** Bisected square

0904. Apply the instructions below to Fig. 22.

Start in the top left corner, go down 1 dot, diagonal right and down 1 dot, right 1 dot, up 1 dot, left 1 dot, diagonal right and up 1 dot.

Where did you end?

    A. Top row, third dot
    B. Second row, second dot
    C. Second row, third dot
    D. Top row, second dot

FIGURE 23

0905. Review Fig. 23. How many red buttons are there?

    A. Four   **C.** Six
    B. Two   **D.** Five

0906. Review Fig. 23. How many buttons have four holes?

    A. Four   **C.** Ten
    B. Six   **D.** Eight

0907. Review Fig. 23. How many different types of buttons are there? Each color with a different number of holes (either two or four) is a type of button.

    A. Eleven   **C.** Twelve
    B. Nine   **D.** Five

0908. Review Fig. 23. How many buttons have two holes?

    A. Eight   **C.** Twelve
    B. Ten   **D.** Thirteen

0909. Review Fig. 23. How many total button holes are there?

    A. Forty   **C.** Thirty-six
    B. Forty-four   **D.** Thirty-two

0910. Review Fig. 23. How many total buttons are there?

    A. Twelve   **C.** Eighteen
    B. Thirteen   **D.** Fourteen

0911. How many tools are pictured below?

    A. Twelve
    B. Ten
    C. Eight
    D. Eleven

FIGURE 24

0912. You are making a necklace. If you continue to string the beads following the pattern in Fig. 24, which color bead should come next?

    A. Red   **C.** Blue
    B. Yellow   **D.** Green

0913. If you continue to string the beads following the pattern in Fig. 24, which color bead would come twelfth?

    A. Yellow   **C.** Blue
    B. Red   **D.** Green

0914. If you continue to string the beads following the pattern in Fig. 24, which color bead would come seventeenth?

    A. Red   **C.** Yellow
    B. Blue   **D.** Green

0915. Based on the beads in Fig. 24, if you add green to your pattern between the yellow and the blue bead, what color bead would come eleventh?

    A. Red   **C.** Blue
    B. Yellow   **D.** Green

0916. Review the grouped symbols shown below. Which symbol does *not* belong in the group?

    A   B   C   D

    A. D   **C.** A
    B. C   **D.** B

0917. How many total strands of hair are in the ponytail shown at right?

A. Seven   C. Eight
B. Six   D. Nine

0918. How many total strands of hair are in the beard shown at right?

A. Nine   C. Ten
B. Eight   D. Seven

FIGURE 25

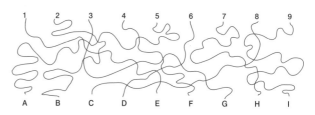

0919. Review Fig. 25. Which number is connected to the letter "I"?

A. 5   C. 8
B. 6   D. 9

0920. Review Fig. 25. Which number is connected to the letter "E"?

A. 6   C. 1
B. 4   D. 3

0921. Review Fig. 25. To which letter does the number 5 connect?

A. D   C. C
B. B   D. A

0922. Review Fig. 25. What do the numbers 4-5-8-1 spell using the letters to which they are connected?

A. FACE   C. ACED
B. HIDE   D. BADE

0923. Review Fig. 25. How many times does line 2 cross line 3?

    A. Two   **C.** Five
    B. Three   **D.** One

FIGURE 26

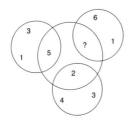

0924. In Fig. 26, which number should go where the "?" is?

    A. 1   **C.** 2
    B. 3   **D.** 4

0925. In Fig. 26, how many intersections are there?

    A. Seven   **C.** Six
    B. Five   **D.** Four

0926. What word is shown at right?

    A. June   **C.** Unit
    B. New   **D.** Done

FIGURE 27

0927. Based on Fig. 27, what is the sum of the numbers?

    A. 20   **C.** 19
    B. 24   **D.** 27

0928. Based on Fig. 27, what are the numbers in numerical order?

    A. 1, 2, 4, 8, 9   **C.** 1, 3, 5, 7, 8
    B. 1, 3, 4, 7, 9   **D.** 1, 2, 3, 4, 5

FIGURE 28

0929. Review Fig. 28. Which animal does *not* belong?

    A. Fox   **C.** Rooster
    B. Pig   **D.** Cow

0930. Review Fig. 28. How many different types of cows are there?

    A. Four   **C.** Three
    B. Five   **D.** Two

0931. Review Fig. 28. How many total eggs are there?

    A. Thirteen   **C.** Twelve
    B. Ten   **D.** Eleven

0932. Review Fig. 28. How many eggs did each egg-laying animal lay?

    A. Six   **C.** Four
    B. Three   **D.** Five

0933. Review Fig. 28. Which animal shown in the figure is typically known as being sly?

    A. Fox   **C.** Pigs
    B. Goats   **D.** Sheep

0934. Review Fig. 28. How many animals have hooves?

    A. Sixteen   **C.** Seventeen
    B. Eighteen   **D.** Fifteen

0935. The figure shown at right was made using six blocks. Which of the following blocks was *not* used to make the figure?

A.   B.   C.   D.

0936. In the diagram shown at right, how many boxes make up the cube?

A. Sixty-four   C. Sixty-two
B. Forty-eight   D. Forty-two

0937. If the small coffee cup holds 2 ounces of coffee, approximately how many ounces of coffee can the big coffee cup hold?

A. 12 ounces
B. 9 ounces
C. 18 ounces
D. 14 ounces

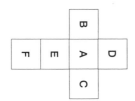

FIGURE 29

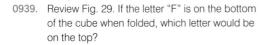

0938. Which of the following cubes is the same as the unfolded cube in Fig. 29?

A.   C.

B.   D.

0939. Review Fig. 29. If the letter "F" is on the bottom of the cube when folded, which letter would be on the top?

A. B   C. E
B. D   D. A

0940. Is it possible to make the figure shown above using the four blocks below? You may *not* rotate the blocks.

    A. Yes
    B. No

0941. How many total shapes were used to make the figure shown at right?

    A. Six   **C.** Five
    B. Seven   **D.** Eight

0942. Which shape was used more than once to create the figure shown at right?

    A. Circle   **C.** Triangle
    B. Square   **D.** Diamond

0943. How many total triangles are in the picture shown at right?

    A. Ten   **C.** Eight
    B. Nine   **D.** Eleven

0944. How many intersections are there in the diagram shown at right?

    A. Eleven   **C.** Thirteen
    B. Twelve   **D.** Ten

FIGURE 30

0945. Which three of the following boxes shown below will create Fig. 30 when superimposed on top of each other? You cannot rotate the boxes.

    1   2   3   4   5

    A. 3, 5, 1   **C.** 2, 3, 4
    B. 1, 2, 3   **D.** 2, 5, 1

FIGURE 31   **FIGURE 32**

0946. Which of the pieces shown below is *not* a part of Fig. 31?

A.   B.   C.    D.

0947. Which of the pieces shown below is *not* a part of Fig. 32?

A.   B.   C.   D.

0948. Which part of the clock shown at right is incorrect?

A. One of the numbers
B. The hands
C. The face
D. The number of ticks

0949. What element is missing from the picture shown at right?

A. Pad   **C.** Buttons
B. Wheel   **D.** Hand

0950. To complete the pattern below, which symbol should appear next?

        ?

A.   C.

B.   D.

0951. What is the first letter of the word that represents what is wrong with the door shown at right?

A. H   **C.** K
B. W   **D.** D

FIGURE 33

EXERCISE MORE THAN YOUR BRAIN

Physical exercise can improve mental faculties. As exercise converts fat to muscle and strengthens the heart, it also stimulates the nervous system. Endorphins, like serotonin and dopamine, are released during physical activity, elevating your mood and improving attention, clarity of thought, and morale. In return, your mental capabilities strengthen and increase.

1   2

4   3

0952. In Fig. 33, what shape is hidden in section 1?

A. A star   **C.** A diamond
B. A heart   **D.** Nothing

0953. In Fig. 33, which number is hidden in section 2?

A. 7   **C.** 9
B. 5   **D.** 1

0954. In Fig. 33, in which section is the number 9 hidden?

A. 2   **C.** 1
B. 3   **D.** 4

0955. In Fig. 33, what is hidden in section 4?

A. The number 8   **C.** A circle
B. A diamond   **D.** Nothing

0956. In Fig. 33, how many times do you see a number 7 in section 2?

A. Three   **C.** Two
B. Four   **D.** One

0957. In Fig. 33, in which section is the letter "A" hidden?

    A. 4   **C.** 3
    B. 2   **D.** 1

0958. Say the *color* of each of the following words out loud and keep track of the number of times you made a mistake.

GREEN BLUE RED BLACK YELLOW BLUE BLACK RED GREEN
BLUE RED YELLOW BLACK GREEN RED BLUE YELLOW BLACK

How many mistakes did you make?

    A. 0–1   **C.** 4–5
    B. 2–3   **D.** 6 or more

0959. How many total triangles are in the figure shown at right?

    A. Seventeen   **C.** Twenty-seven
    B. Sixteen   **D.** Twenty-one

0960. The image shown at right represents what?

    A. A type of ice cream
    B. A type of word font
    C. A mammal
    D. A place

0961. Which of the following numbers is the same as the number above?

    A. 21507527827   **C.** 17578512087
    B. 72810753719   **D.** 21587282751

0962. What word(s) does the picture shown at right represent?

    A. Lucky pair   **C.** High roller
    B. Paradise   **D.** Gambling

FIGURE 34

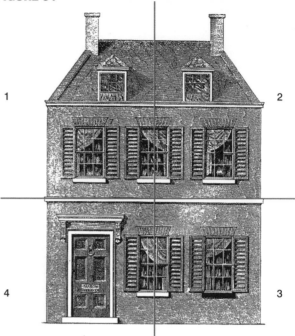

1

2

4

3

0963. In Fig. 34, what lucky item is hidden in section 1?

A. Four-leaf clover **C.** Rabbit's foot
B. $ **D.** 7

0964. In Fig. 34, what is missing in section 2?

A. Nothing   **C.** Curtain
B. Shutter bar   **D.** Window grid

0965. In Fig. 34, what is missing from section 4?

A. Curtain   **C.** Door knob
B. Window pane   **D.** Door panel

0966. In Fig. 34, how is section 3 different from the other sections?

A. There are two curtains
B. There isn't a curtain
C. Bottom of window is dark
D. The design above the window is different

0967. Compare the two pictures shown below. How is the picture on the right different?

    A. Cross by arm removed
    B. Cross at necklace removed
    C. Flower colored in
    D. Top of scepter missing

0968. Based on the pattern shown below, which shapes would be in "C"?

    A. ●●▲■■   **C.** ●●▲▲■
    B. ●▲▲■■   **D.** ●●▲▲■■

FIGURE 35

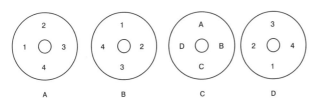

0969. Based on Fig. 35, what number should go where the letter "C" is on tire C?

    A. 4   **C.** 1
    B. 3   **D.** 2

0970. Based on Fig. 35, what is the sum of "D" and "B" on tire C?

    A. 3   **C.** 6
    B. 4   **D.** 5

FIGURE 36

0971. In Fig. 36, how many apples are red?

    A. Sixteen   **C.** Thirteen
    B. Seventeen   **D.** Fifteen

0972. In Fig. 36, how many apples are yellow?

    A. Nine   **C.** Eleven
    B. Ten   **D.** Twelve

0973. In Fig. 36, how many stars are disguised in section 1?

    A. Three   **C.** Four
    B. Two   **D.** One

0974. In Fig. 36, what's hidden in section 2?

    A. Star   **C.** Bird
    B. Question mark **D.** Nothing

0975. You have one minute to review Fig. 36. Press the ⏻ on the Coach, then answer the question as quickly as you can. [STOP] What's missing from the picture?

    A. Ears of animals
    B. Man's hat
    C. Man's hand in section 2
    D. Man's foot

0976. In Fig. 36, the tree's leaves are falling. How many have hit the ground?

A. Three
C. Five
B. Four
D. None

FIGURE 37

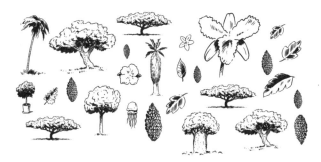

0977. Review Fig. 37. How many palm trees are there?

A. Two
C. Three
B. One
D. Four

0978. Review Fig. 37. Which object does *not* belong in the picture?

A. Potted tree
C. Jellyfish
B. Palm frond
D. Pinecone

0979. Review Fig. 37. How many total trees are there?

A. Eight
C. Seven
B. Ten
D. Nine

0980. Review the unfolded cube shown at right. If the yellow circle is at the top of the cube when it is folded, what will be on the bottom?

A. A red square
C. A blue circle
B. A red circle
D. A blue square

0981. Into what classification does the word shown at right fall?

A. Animal
C. Vegetable
B. Fruit
D. Mineral

TAKE CARE OF YOUR BRAIN

Taking care of the brain, like any other part of your body, can be done with proper diet, hydration, and exercise. Laughing, loving, working, and playing are also important factors in maintaining good mental and physical health, each, of course, with proper moderation. It's also important to get adequate sleep and to limit your intake of drugs and alcohol. Most importantly, keeping a balanced and healthy lifestyle will help you maintain good cognitive functioning.

236

0982. What is the order of apple trees shown below according to harvest seasons?

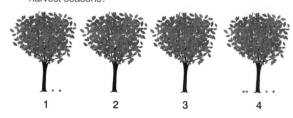

1   2   3   4

A. 3, 2, 4, 1   **C.** 3, 1, 4, 2
B. 2, 3, 1, 4   **D.** 1, 4, 3, 2

0983. The mirror image of the time shown at right is what?

A. 10:05   **C.** 1:25
B. 5:05   **D.** 10:35

0984. The mirror image of the time shown at right is what?

A. 1:25   **C.** 11:25
B. 4:05   **D.** 10:40

0985. The mirror image of the time shown at right is what?

A. 1:50   **C.** 7:40
B. 4:20   **D.** 2:40

0986. The mirror image of the time shown at right is what?

A. 7:40   **C.** 4:45
B. 2:45   **D.** 10:45

FIGURE 38

0987. Which of the following squares would perfectly overlap the blue square in Fig. 38?

A.   **B.**   **C.**   **D.**

FIGURE 39

1 2

4 3

0988. In Fig. 39, which square is the "luckiest"?

    A. Section 3   **C.** Section 2
    B. Section 1   **D.** Section 4

0989. In Fig. 39, how many Z's are hidden in section 2?

    A. Six   **C.** Five
    B. Three   **D.** Four

0990. In Fig. 39, how many 7s are hidden in the picture?

    A. Fifteen   **C.** Fourteen
    B. Twelve   **D.** Eleven

0991. In Fig. 39, what is missing in section 3?

    A. "I" in Favorite   **C.** Passengers
    B. Lug nut   **D.** Nothing

0992. In Fig. 39, what item is hidden in all sections?

    A. Z's   **C.** 7's
    B. Circles   **D.** I's

0993. In Fig. 39, how many circles are hidden in section 4?

    A. Two   **C.** One
    B. Three   **D.** None

FIGURE 40

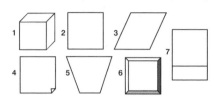

0994. Which of the following three shapes comprise Fig. 40?

A. 1, 4, 5   **C.** 1, 5, 7
B. 2, 5, 7   **D.** 1, 2, 5

0995. My image is the same both right-side-up and upside-down. I am a close relative, but upside down I am a synonym of knockout and an antonym of flop. I am your what?

A. Father   **C.** Sister
B. Mother   **D.** Brother

0996. Review the triangles shown below. Which distance is longer, A to B or B to C?

A. B to C
B. A to B
C. They are the same distance

0997. Where should the shadow fall in the picture shown at right?

A. To the left and front of the house
B. Directly in front of the house
C. To the right of the house
D. Behind the house

FIGURE 41

0998. In Fig. 41, which spider is missing a leg?

    A. 11   **C.** 12
    B. 6   **D.** 1

0999. In Fig. 41, which two spiders are identical?

    A. 5 and 15   **C.** 1 and 10
    B. 5 and 11   **D.** 7 and 13

1000. In Fig. 41, which spider is dotted-jointed?

    A. 15   **C.** 8
    B. 13   **D.** 4

1001. In Fig. 41, how many total legs are there?

    A. 119   **C.** 120
    B. 89   **D.** 90

CONCLUSION

Congratulations! You have completed a major undertaking by taking charge of your cognitive health. You have dedicated yourself to the extraordinary task of improving the speed, efficiency, and accuracy of your thinking. Regardless of the level at which you started, or even the level at which you ended, by working through this program, you have made substantial advancements in your cognitive growth. And it is essential that you continue with your commitment to your mind.

We encourage you to continue utilizing the *Brain Boot Camp*. This program is a powerful tool and offers you the ability to continue working and reworking exercises. If you are feeling disorganized or are having difficulty thinking through a task, then work some questions in the Organization, Planning, and Logic section. Are you forgetting things you normally would remember? Then, brush up your temporal lobes by completing some Memory exercises. Also, review the beginnings of each chapter, which discusses how each part of the brain works, and the helpful hints and information located throughout the book. Whichever mode you work in, questions you answer, or tips you read, the essential element here is effort.

We encourage you to challenge yourself to achieve your optimum level of brain health. Faster, more efficient thinking means better quality of life, both for you and for the others around you. Take college courses, discover new hobbies, learn to write with both hands simultaneously, or visit a foreign country and get a new job; love and play to your fullest potential. Each minute of each day is an opportunity to grow.

Remember, your brain is constantly changing. With each new experience, new neural pathways are established, increasing the density of your brain's structure and the complexity of its functions, and thus reducing its susceptibility to damage and disease. We encourage you to continue creating more pathways to maintain the intricate architecture and vast circuitry within your brain.

By completing *Brain Boot Camp*, you have made considerable strides in improving your brain-power. It's important to keep making the efforts necessary to maintain a healthy brain for the rest of your life! So, for the brain's sake, and yours, continue to live life to the fullest. We wish you the very best, and may all of your memories remain content.

ABOUT THE AUTHORS

Douglas J. Mason, PsyD, is a neuropsychologist in private practice. He currently works in the evaluation and treatment of patients with cognitive disorders. He completed his postdoctoral training in neuropsychology at Duke University and his internship at the Memphis VA and the University of Tennessee.

Brenda Mason holds a master's degree in business administration and has worked for Fortune 500 companies and the Duke University Medical Center.

ACKNOWLEDGMENTS

We are grateful for the effort and hard work of those who have contributed to this book. First and foremost, we'd like to thank Rose Burdge for her continued stellar performance. Sincere thanks to Joan Lourenco and Sheena Allman for their contributions. It was a great pleasure working with our fine editors, Amelia Riedler and Matthew Taylor—thank you for your guidance and patience.

DEDICATION

This book is dedicated to our beautiful daughters, Stephanie, Jenna, and Jordyn. Thank you, Papaw, for helping with the girls.